LCVP LINK MODU

GW00360722

MAKING IT HAPPEN

by Caroline McHale

Folens

Editor
Frieda Donohoe

Design and Layout
Karen Hoey

Cover Design
Karen Hoey

Illustrations
Gary Dermody
Olivia Golden
Karen Hoey
Claire Kavanagh
Bronagh O'Hanlon

Photographer
Declan Corrigan

© Caroline McHale 2005

ISBN 1-84131-699-7

Folens Publishers
Hibernian Industrial Estate,
Greenhills Road,
Tallaght,
Dublin 24.

The author and publisher wish to thank the following for permission to reproduce copyright material.
Aer Arann, Alamy, AWARE, Business 2000, Celtic Enterprise Programme, Department of the Environment, Heritage and Local Government, FÁS, Getty Images, the Global Entrepreneurship Monitor, Imagestate, John Walmsley (Education Photos), Kildare County Enterprise Board, the NCCA, Photocall Ireland, SIPTU, The Society of St Vincent de Paul in Ireland, the State Exams Commission and Trócaire.
Thanks also to the LCVP Support Service (see pp. 17, 91, 97–9, 143 and 172–4) for materials adapted from the LCVP Support Service booklets).

MAKING IT HAPPEN: LCVP LINK MODULES

	Things to Keep in Mind	Guidelines for Structure	Templates for Rough Work	Mind Maps	Sample Portfolio Items
CORE PORTFOLIO ITEMS					
CV	p. 78	p. 79	pp. 80–81		p. 82
Career Investigation	p. 101	pp. 102–03	pp. 104–05	p. 106	p. 107–08
Summary Report	p. 19	p. 20	p. 21, p. 33, p. 36		p. 22
Enterprise/Action Plan	p. 5	p. 6	p. 7	p. 8	p. 9
OPTIONAL PORTFOLIO ITEMS					
Diary of Work Experience	p. 122	p. 123	p. 124–30	p. 131	p. 132-5
Enterprise Report	p. 202	p. 203	p. 204–05	p. 206	p. 207–09
Recorded Interview/Presentation	p. 24	p. 28	p. 26, p. 29		
Report on 'My Own Place'	p. 56	p. 57	p. 58–9	p. 60	

Activities	The PEP Appproach	Guidelines/Layout	Templates for Rough Work	Checklists	Quizzes	Evaluation	Sample Items
Visit In	pp. 30-1		p. 33	p. 32		pp. 14–15	
Visit Out	p. 34		p. 36	p. 35		pp. 14–15	
Job Interview	p. 83						
Other Interviews			p. 99, pp. 145–6				
Characteristics of an Entrepreneur					pp. 147–8		
Strengths and Weaknesses		p. 168	p. 143		pp. 92–95		p. 169
Cross-curricular links		p. 16	p. 17, p. 98				
Applying for a job	pp. 69–70, p. 83	p. 73	p. 71, pp. 75–6				p. 72
Skills Audit					p. 91		
Work Placement	p. 116					p. 15 pp.118–21	
'My Own Place' Investigation			pp. 40–42			p. 15	
Questionnaires		p. 195	pp. 172–4				p. 197
Profile of a Voluntary Organisation/Community Enterprise			pp. 185–6				

Assessment	NCCA Recommendations	Comparison of Reports	Marks	Format	Method
Exam			p. 215	pp. 216–17	
Portfolio	p. 218	p. 219	p. 215, pp. 220-21		
Case Study					pp. 224–6

INTRODUCTION

This book is divided into **four** distinct sections and can be used in whatever order you prefer. You don't have to adhere to the book rigidly as you may opt to engage in different activities and select the relevant information as required in order to achieve the syllabus outcomes, which are documented as **S**pecific **L**earning **O**utcomes (SLOs).

The **L**eaving **C**ertificate **V**ocational **P**rogramme (**LCVP**) is a senior cycle programme designed to give a strong vocational dimension to the Leaving Certificate. The focus of the LCVP is to prepare you for adult life by ensuring you are educated in the broadest sense possible. It will help you to develop the ability to cope and thrive in a work environment of rapid change. The programme gears you towards self-directed learning, being innovative and enterprising and acquiring attitudes and skills appropriate to the world of work.

The programme is divided into **two Link Modules**, which are best fostered through involvement in **activity–based** learning. All activities should be broken down into three distinct phases: **P**re-experience, **E**xperience and **P**ost-experience (**PEP**) or before, during and after. The Link Modules are designed to make connections between the school and the community, future study and careers, enterprise and setting up a business.

LINK MODULES

1. PREPARATION FOR THE WORLD OF WORK

2. ENTERPRISE EDUCATION

The two **Link Modules** are short courses and are treated as **one** for assessment purposes, which is at a common level.

Requirements for the LCVP

- ✿ You must take a minimum of five Leaving Certificate subjects.
- ✿ Two of the above must be selected from the designated **V**ocational **S**ubject **G**roupings (**VSGs**).
- ✿ You must follow a recognised course in a **modern European language**.
- ✿ You must study two **Link Modules** – Preparation for the World of Work and Enterprise Education.

Activities and Skills you will develop in the LCVP

LCVP LINK MODULES – Two Link Modules

PREPARATION FOR THE WORLD OF WORK

This module is designed to develop your general understanding of the world of work, to introduce you to career research and provide you with the knowledge and skills to find employment. As part of this module, you are expected to complete a Career Investigation and engage in work experience or in a work shadow placement.

The module is divided into **four units**:

1. Introduction to Working Life
2. Job-seeking Skills
3. Career Investigation
4. Work Placement

ENTERPRISE EDUCATION

This module aims to develop creativity, resourcefulness, self-confidence and initiative. You are encouraged to interview enterprising people, investigate local enterprises and set up your own enterprise projects as vehicles of learning.

The module is divided into **four units**:

1. Enterprise Skills
2. Local Business Enterprises
3. Local Voluntary Organisations/Community Enterprises
4. An Enterprise Activity

The syllabus is divided into Learning Outcomes. There are **93 S**pecific **L**earning **O**utcomes (**SLOs**).

Preparation for the World of Work	**44 SLOs**
Enterprise Education	**49 SLOs**

There are some SLOs repeated throughout the syllabus, e.g. 'Link the learning to Leaving Certificate subjects', 'Evaluate activities', 'Planning', 'Report writing', 'Invite a visitor to the classroom' etc.

The Specific Learning Outcomes are documented at the beginning of each of the eight units. This book is a mixture of activities, templates and sufficient content to ensure that you are adequately prepared for the written paper. Use the templates to document key words, then revisit and elaborate on them prior to submission. Remember, the written exam is in the form of a booklet, quite similar to some of the activities in this book.

When writing portfolio entries, make sure that you follow the important assessment guidelines and assessment criteria. This book has samples of portfolio items but make sure that the portfolio entries **you submit are your own individual work**, otherwise you may be penalised. As you participate in all of the activities, make sure you have individual evidence of your own work and make sure that your work is not identical to that of others. Remember, when deciding what to submit for your portfolio, you're expected to review all your work and pick the **best six items**.

This book contains detailed information on all portfolio items – the four mandatory core items and the four optional items.

The last section of this book deals with assessment, offering additional advice and guidelines.

Finally, I hope you find this book useful as you participate in the programme. Wishing you every success in the future. Good luck and enjoy.

Caroline McHale 2005

ACKNOWLEDGEMENTS

This book is designed to embody the best of my experience, as both a support person and a teacher of LCVP. It gives a clear and concise guide to the LCVP Link Modules and will be of great value to both teachers and students.

This book could not have been produced without the help of the past and present LCVP Support Service and the Second Level Support Service. It was a privilege to work with the Department of Education and Science and I would like, in particular, to acknowledge the LCVP team I worked with, who brought great clarity to the revised Link Modules Syllabus. I would also like to thank the many teachers I have been privileged to work with while leading in-service sessions. Their comments and suggestions on the LCVP were invaluable.

I would like to acknowledge the NCCA for their clear guidelines on the assessment of the revised Link Modules, which have helped enormously in drafting portfolio entries and assessment questions.

Sincere thanks to John O'Connor and to all the staff at Folens, in particular Frieda Donohue who was enthusiastic, encouraging and fantastic to work with. Karen Hoey's colourful and professional designs have also added greatly to the book.

I wish also to acknowledge the support of my colleagues, friends and especially my family who have been so patient, encouraging and understanding with me over the last few months.

Last but not least, I wish to thank the staff and students of Presentation De La Salle College, Bagenalstown, Co. Carlow, in particular my LCVP students who tried and tested many of the innovations, activities and questions that I have included in this book.

**This book is dedicated to my parents
Margaret and Peter McHale.**

An Outline of the LCVP Link Modules Mind Map

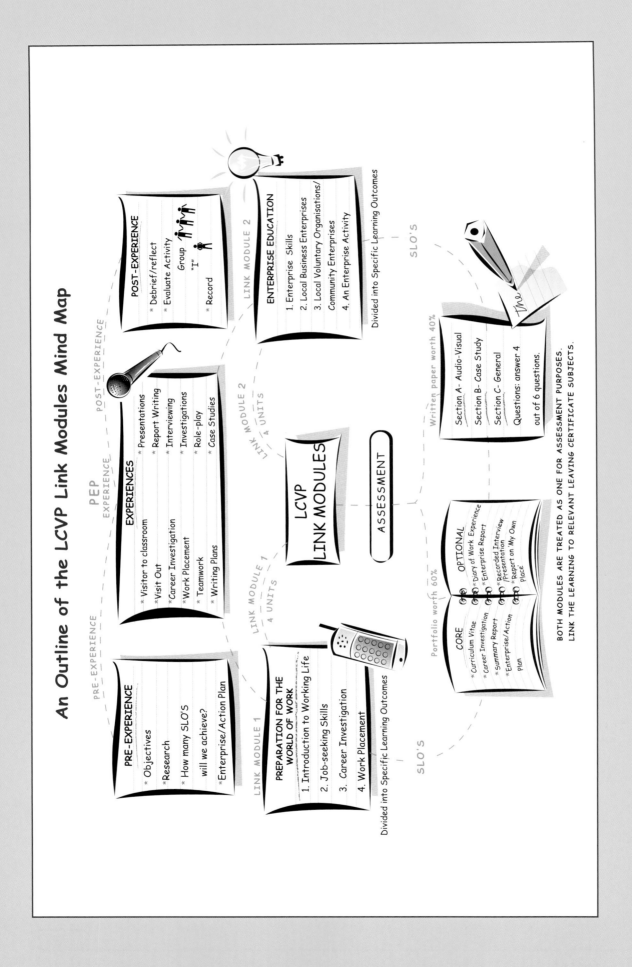

PRE-EXPERIENCE

PEP
EXPERIENCE

POST-EXPERIENCE

PRE-EXPERIENCE
* Objectives
* Research
* How many SLO'S will we achieve?
* Enterprise/Action Plan

EXPERIENCES
* Visitor to classroom   * Presentations
* Visit Out   * Report Writing
* Career Investigation   * Interviewing
* Work Placement   * Investigations
* Teamwork   * Role-play
* Writing Plans   * Case Studies

POST-EXPERIENCE
* Debrief/reflect
* Evaluate Activity
  Group
  "I"
* Record

LINK MODULE 2

ENTERPRISE EDUCATION
1. Enterprise Skills
2. Local Business Enterprises
3. Local Voluntary Organisations/
   Community Enterprises
4. An Enterprise Activity

Divided into Specific Learning Outcomes

LINK MODULE 2
4 UNITS

LINK MODULE 1
4 UNITS

LCVP LINK MODULES

ASSESSMENT

LINK MODULE 1

PREPARATION FOR THE WORLD OF WORK
1. Introduction to Working Life
2. Job-seeking Skills
3. Career Investigation
4. Work Placement

Divided into Specific Learning Outcomes

SLO'S

Written paper worth 40%

Section A- Audio-Visual
Section B- Case Study
Section C- General
Questions: answer 4
out of 6 questions.

Portfolio worth 60%

CORE
* Curriculum Vitae
* Career Investigation
* Summary Report
* Enterprise/Action Plan

OPTIONAL
* Diary of Work Experience
* Enterprise Report
* Recorded Interview Presentation
* Report on 'My Own Place'

BOTH MODULES ARE TREATED AS ONE FOR ASSESSMENT PURPOSES.
LINK THE LEARNING TO RELEVANT LEAVING CERTIFICATE SUBJECTS.

SLO'S

SECTION 1: PEP - AN INTEGRATED LEARNING APPROACH

AN INTRODUCTION TO PEP: PRE-EXPERIENCE, EXPERIENCE AND POST-EXPERIENCE

The aim of this section is to help you to develop an integrated approach to your study of the Link Modules. Throughout your two-year LCVP experience, you will participate in many different activities – visiting enterprises/organisations, inviting people to speak to your class, doing a work placement etc. This book will help you to approach these activities in such a way that you will learn and gain as much as you possibly can from each of them. This book outlines processes and procedures that can be applied to every activity you undertake, ensuring that you can easily use those activities to prepare your portfolio items and get ready for assessment.

Each activity in this book can be broken up into 3 **PEP** parts: **P**re-experience, **E**xperience and **P**ost-experience or before, during and after.

In order to make each experience as rich and as useful as possible, you should always start by preparing for the activity, move on to participating in the activity and finish by evaluating it.

As you will see from the diagram on the next page, there is as much, if not more, work required of students before and after the experience as during it.

Remember, you must take responsibility for your own learning.

- ✿ **Plan** your experience.
- ✿ **Participate** in your experience.
- ✿ **Reflect** on and **evaluate** your experience.
- ✿ **Record** learning.

Note: Keep an **LCVP folder** and record your learning using templates and ideas demonstrated in this book. After two years using this book and the templates and activities in it, you will be adequately prepared for the assessment.

Use the templates to document key words, revisit and elaborate upon them and record them in your **LCVP folder**. As you word-process your portfolio entries, make sure they are **error free – perfect**.

PLAN
- Decide how many SLOs you want to achieve.
- Decide on objectives and aims.
- Do research.
- Draw up a timetable.
- Use Enterprise/Action Plan template.

LCVP Activities
- Career Investigation
- Planning
- Visit In/Visit Out
- Report writing
- Work placement (work experience/work shadow)
- Enterprise Activities
- Interviews/Investigations
- Presentations

PRE-EXPERIENCE

EXPERIENCE

PEP

POST-EXPERIENCE

EXPERIENCE/ ACTIVITY
- Participate actively in the activity. Do not be an onlooker.

RECORD
- Use templates.
- Use your LCVP folder.
- Write reports.
- Prepare a Recorded Interview/Presentation.

EVALUATE
1. **Debrief**: Reflect on the experience.
2. **Assess**
   (a) The activity
   (b) Personal performance
   (c) Group performance
   (d) Cross-curricular links
3. **Conclude and Recommend**
   (a) Draw conclusions.
   (b) Make recommendations based on your conclusions.
   (c) Suggest follow-on activities.

PRE-EXPERIENCE

Participating in an activity that you have prepared for is a far more rewarding experience than participating in one that you have not prepared for. When you are prepared, you feel more confident, you know what it is you want to get from the experience and you have already come up with ideas on how you're going to do that. Preparing guarantees not only that you'll enjoy the experience more, but also that you will gain more from it.

PLAN
- Decide how many SLOs you want to achieve.
- Decide on objectives and aims.
- Do research.
- Draw up a timetable.
- Use Enterprise/Action Plan template.

Plan

'A plan without action is a dream; action without a plan is a nightmare.'

Chinese proverb

The ability to **plan** effectively is a useful skill in most situations. Consider the following:
- ✿ The ability to plan can help you at school, at home and in the community.
- ✿ Preparing for future studies is easier if you have some experience of planning and research.
- ✿ Planning skills are important when you are looking for a job.
- ✿ If you want to start your own business, the ability to plan ahead is essential.

What is a Plan?

- ✿ A plan refers to an activity, which **may** take place in the future.
- ✿ It is a **series of steps** to be taken in order to achieve aims or objectives.
- ✿ It is a **written** document.

As an LCVP student, you must be aware of and understand two kinds of plans.
1. **A Business Plan**: This comes up in the written examination only.
2. **An Enterprise/Action Plan**: This comes up as a core portfolio item **and/or** can come up in the written examination.

Reasons to Prepare a Plan

- ✪ It helps you to make informed decisions based on careful research and analysis.
- ✪ It gives you a focus for the future.
- ✪ It establishes targets and describes how to achieve those targets.
- ✪ It identifies the resources needed.
- ✪ It raises questions and anticipates solutions.
- ✪ It analyses **S**trengths, **W**eaknesses, **O**pportunities and **T**hreats (**SWOT**).
- ✪ It provides a benchmark (a standard to compare against) for evaluating performances.
- ✪ It is an essential requirement when applying for bank loans and grants.
- ✪ It can indicate whether you should **go ahead** with your idea or **stop**.

Planning for LCVP Activities

Before starting any of the LCVP activities, it is important to take the time to do some **P**re-experience work to prepare for them. You should go through the following steps in preparation for each experience:

1. Ask yourself what the **S**pecific **L**earning **O**utcomes for that activity are? What are you expected to learn from the experience?
2. Is there anything not included in the **S**pecific **L**earning **O**utcomes that you can learn from the activity?
3. Make sure that you understand the assessment criteria for both the portfolio and the written paper, so that you can make sure that you do everything you need to do and learn everything that you are expected to learn.
4. Plan how you will evaluate links to Leaving Cert subjects, activities, teamwork and 'My Contribution'.

Enterprise/Action Plan

One of your core portfolio items is the Enterprise/Action Plan. You can produce an Enterprise/Action Plan for any one of a number of activities and then submit it as a portfolio item. Even if you don't intend submitting an Enterprise/Action Plan for a particular activity you are planning, you will find that the Enterprise/Action Plan templates and guidelines can still help you to structure it.

  The next few pages are dedicated to walking you through the preparation of an Enterprise/Action Plan and, once you have attempted this plan, you will find planning in general a much easier task. An Enterprise/Action Plan starts with documenting your objectives/aims – what you hope to achieve from this activity, both as a group and as an individual. You must next decide on suitable methods of research and do the research. This process will highlight any challenges and help you to decide whether you should go ahead with the activity. Then, decide on the tasks that both you and the group must complete to implement the plan and estimate the time needed to complete them. Once you have decided on a timetable, you can identify what resources you will need, e.g. financial resources, and you can decide how you will raise the required finance. Finally, you must decide in advance how you will evaluate the activity, i.e. how you will determine if you have achieved your objectives. Remember, these steps can be followed when planning any activity, even if you don't intend submitting an Enterprise/Action Plan for it. In fact, it is a good idea to prepare an Enterprise/Action Plan for every activity.

PORTFOLIO ITEM: ENTERPRISE/ACTION PLAN

'Failed business did not plan to fail but failed to plan.'

In the LCVP you may decide to plan lots of activities. You do not have to do all the activities you plan, but you must do the research. Remember the Enterprise/Action Plan is for an enterprise activity or some other action that you intend to do in the LCVP. The action must be related to one or more of the **S**pecific **L**earning **O**utcomes (SLOs).

The following are opportunities in the LCVP to prepare a plan:
* A plan for a **'My Own Place'** investigation
* A plan for a **Visit In**
* A plan for a **Visit Out**
* A plan for **learning a new skill**
* A plan for a **Work Placement**
* A plan for an **Enterprise Activity**
* A plan for a **Career Investigation**
* A plan for a **Careers Evening**

Note: The **SLOs** offer lots of possibilities for generating Enterprise/Action Plans. Planning a birthday party would not, however, be acceptable!

Things to keep in mind

* Compulsory: In the portfolio, you must submit **six** items. An Enterprise/Action Plan is part of the **mandatory** core.
* The Enterprise/Action Plan must be presented as a word-processed document (300–600 words long).
* The plan must be written in the **future tense**, e.g. 'We will …'
* You must also show evidence that you have conducted research. The analysis of the research is in the **past tense**, e.g. 'We checked the Internet…'
* Use simple language, short sentences and short paragraphs.
* Arrange information under clear headings and bulleted points.
* If you have worked in a group to develop an Enterprise/Action Plan, you must show your **individual contribution**, e.g. if you have a personal objective or a personal research method, refer back to it, ensuring that you present your individual point of view in your analysis and evaluation.
* Use a regular font, such as Times New Roman, size 12pt.
* Keep to a small number of font sizes, e.g. two.

Core
Submit all 4
Optional
Submit 2 out of 4
A total of **6 portfolio items** must be submitted.

Assessment Criteria – Syllabus

The Enterprise/Action Plan will assess your ability to:
* Generate a document with a clear and consistent layout.
* Set objectives.
* Select and conduct relevant research.
* Analyse the results of selected research.
* Devise a logical plan of action.
* Identify and quantify required resources.
* Estimate required time and costs.
* Propose methods by which the success of the plan will be measured.

Tip: Plan an activity you're familiar with, e.g. plan a **table quiz** as a fund-raiser for charity.

Enterprise/Action Plan: Guidelines for Plan Structure

1. **Title**: Include a clear title, stating that this is an Enterprise/Action Plan and identifying its purpose, e.g. 'A Plan for a Visit Out by the LCVP students to a college open day.'

2. **Objectives**: State three objectives, that is things that you (and/or your group) expect to achieve and things you (and/or your group) hope to learn through participating in the planned activity. Make sure that at least one objective is your own **personal objective**.

3. **Research Methods**: You should indicate three types of research that have been carried out to develop the plan. If working in a group, include at least one that you carried out alone. Research methods include the following:
   - Writing or telephoning for information
   - Library or Internet search
   - Using a questionnaire
   - Seeking advice from adults or peers

STOP AND DO THE RESEARCH

4. **Analysis of Research**
   - Summarise the outcome of each research method.
   - Record any relevant information that has been obtained and indicate how it will influence the plan.

5. **Actions**
   - Outline steps you will take to implement the plan.
   - Present steps in chronological order, starting with what must be done first.
   - Clearly identify your individual contribution.

6. **Schedule of Time**
   - Indicate how much time different parts of the planned activity will take.
   - Give the dates of any deadlines.

7. **Resources and Costs**
   - Itemise what resources (materials and personnel) you will need.
   - Estimate the costs of those resources.

8. **Evaluation Methods**: This refers to how the student/group plan to evaluate their own success. How will they know if they have achieved their stated objectives? Link these methods to **each stated objective** and make sure that each objective is evaluated, e.g. 'If we achieve our fund-raising target of €500, then we will have achieved our objective.'

*Tip: Analysis of Research is the **only** section written in the **past**.*

Include an element of feedback if possible, e.g. ask your teacher to evaluate your performance.

Enterprise/Action Plan: Possible Template for Rough Work

Title:

Objectives

Research Methods

Analysis of Research

Actions

Schedule of Time

Resources and Costs

Evaluation Methods

Portfolio Tip: Use this template to plan all activities. Use key words initially, then revisit and elaborate on them later, using your LCVP folder. Start to word-process and remember, your portfolio should be error free – perfect.

Tip: Make sure you evaluate each objective.

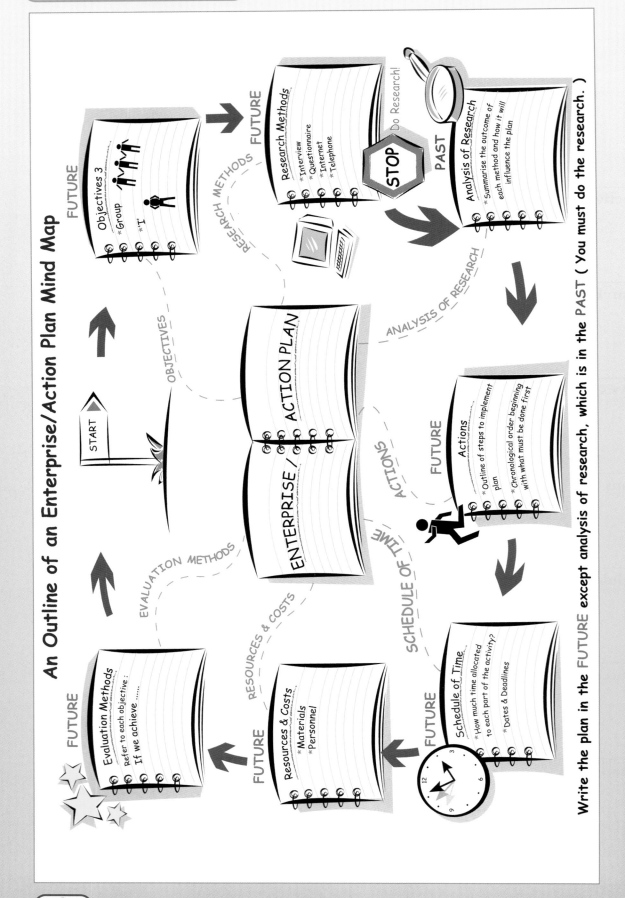

An Outline of an Enterprise/Action Plan Mind Map

Write the plan in the FUTURE except analysis of research, which is in the PAST (You must do the research.)

SAMPLE PORTFOLIO ITEM

ENTERPRISE/ACTION PLAN

PLAN FOR AN LCVP FUNDRAISING EVENT

A plan to organise a school disco to raise money for Trócaire, as part of our enterprise activity for LCVP.

Objectives
- We want to plan an LCVP fundraising activity to raise money for Trócaire.
- We hope that the LCVP class will work well as a team.
- I hope to fulfil part of the LCVP course by doing a personal plan and I hope to improve my planning and organisational skills.

Research Methods
- I will arrange a meeting with our Principal to get permission to hold the disco and to arrange a suitable date, time, D.J. and any other requirements for a disco.
- We will do a survey in school to identify how many students would be interested in attending a school disco.
- I will use the Internet to research modern music tastes and the top 30 singles in Ireland presently.

Analysis of Research
- As a result of my meeting with the Principal, we have permission to hold the disco in the school hall, on Friday, 17th October 2005, from 8 p.m. until 11 p.m. I have arranged for the D.J. Steven Dunford, at a competitive price of €130.
- As a result of our survey, we discovered that out of approximately 450 students in the school, 370 said they will attend a school disco.
- I used the Internet to download the top 30 singles and I hope to continue researching this subject as part of my study of music for my Leaving Certificate.

Actions
- I will ask teachers if they are available to supervise on the night.
- I will confirm D.J. Steven Dunford at our agreed price.
- We will draft and distribute posters around the school.
- We will organise a clean-up in the hall before the disco.
- We must divide up the workload on the night and after the disco.
- We will clean up the hall after the disco.
- I will arrange a meeting with a representative from Trócaire to organise the handing over of the money we will have raised from this LCVP fundraising activity.

Schedule of Time
- **6th October 2005:** I will ask teachers if they are available to supervise the disco.
- **7th October 2005:** I will book the D.J. for that night at the agreed price.
- **9th October 2005:** We will make posters to advertise the disco.
- **16th October 2005:** We will agree on the jobs to be carried out by each member of the group on the night of the disco, e.g. cloakroom, shop.
- **17th October 2005:** Day of the Disco
  - **2.00 p.m.** Clean hall.
  - **3.30 p.m.** Stick tickets beside each hanger in the cloakroom.
  - **7.20 p.m.** Re-open school and help D.J. carry in equipment.
  - **7.45 p.m.** Take floats for front door and cloakroom from shop.
  - **8.00 p.m.** Open doors.
  - **8.30 p.m.** Close doors.
  - **11.00 p.m.** End disco.
  - **11.15 p.m.** Clean up hall.
  - **11.30 p.m.** Once hall is cleaned, have school locked up by caretaker.
- **24th October 2005:** I will arrange a meeting with a Trócaire representative for this day.

Resources and Costs

Resources
- Teachers
- LCVP team

Revenue
Expected revenue from entry fee: €1,500 (300 students at €5 per student, no charge for cloakroom)

Costs

	€130.00
D.J.	€ 7.50
Cloakroom tickets	€ 10.00
Posters	€ 1.20
Phone Calls	
Total	**€148.70**

Proposed money for charity = €1,351.30

Evaluation Methods
- If we raise our target of €1,351.30, then we will have achieved our objective of raising money for Trócaire.
- If we complete this activity according to plan, we will have demonstrated excellent team skills. We will ask our LCVP teacher to evaluate our team and tell us what team skills we demonstrated.
- If this activity runs according to plan, I will have demonstrated my planning and organisational skills. I will ask both my music teacher and the Trócaire representative to comment on both these skills.
- If I can write an Enterprise/Action Plan according to the assessment criteria, I will have achieved my personal objective.
- If we achieve all our objectives, we will have been successful in planning this activity.

EXPERIENCE

LCVP Activities
- Career Investigation
- Planning
- Visit In/Visit Out
- Report writing
- Work placement (work experience/work shadow)
- Enterprise Activities
- Interviews/Investigations
- Presentations

EXPERIENCE/ ACTIVITY
- Participate actively in the activity. Do not be an onlooker.

The Link Modules is a rich, activity-based programme. It offers you many opportunities to plan, organise, and engage in activities both inside and outside the classroom. Activities range from preparing for the world of work by conducting a Career Investigation and/or experiencing a work placement, to taking part in out-of-school visits to a business enterprise, voluntary organisation or community enterprise, to inviting visitors into the classroom. All of these activities give you an opportunity to deal with adults other than teachers. Team activities are also an integral part of the Link Modules and teamwork is particularly important in investigations and enterprise activities.

Regardless of the activity, however, the same integrated learning approach applies. The same steps should be followed in order to ensure that you complete the activity successfully. At the **E**xperience stage of **PEP**, this involves participating actively in whatever it is you are doing and ensuring that you get as much as you possibly can from it. We will now demonstrate how this approach can be applied to Visits Out. The following is a Case Study of a Visit Out to a design company.

Case Study: A Visit Out to Design International Ltd.

The LCVP class went on a visit to Design International Ltd. Unfortunately, due to traffic congestion, they were about ten minutes late for the visit. They were met by the Human Resource Manager, Evelyn Hernon. One of the LCVP students, Sharon, introduced the group and apologised for being late. Sharon seemed very enthusiastic about the visit and she told Evelyn that everybody was really looking forward to hearing all about the company.

During the visit, the students were shown fantastic ceramic sculptures. These, they were told, were produced mostly for the corporate market. Design International Ltd is also willing to design one-off productions for the consumer market. The pieces vary in price from €3,000 to €10,000. Evelyn spoke about the importance of research and development. The sculptures are generally made to the customers' specifications but Design International Ltd will offer design advice if required. In that case, idea generation is very important because customers expect original and unique pieces. Since production comprises mostly of one-off items, very skilled labour is required along with highly specialised equipment. The company is owned by two brothers who initially formed a partnership, but later decided to become a private company in order to ensure limited liability. The company presently employs 40 members of staff. Teamwork is an important aspect of the business, as is training. All employees are encouraged to take and actively engage in training courses.

The company advertises mainly through their website and in business magazines. Initially, they geared their products towards the American market but they have recently entered the European market and have been amazed by the success and the potential of this growing market. They are presently advertising for graduates with foreign languages who would also need to be familiar with ICT (Information and Communications Technology). Video-conferencing is used to communicate with existing clients.

Evelyn was extremely enthusiastic when explaining all of this to the students, but some of the LCVP students were concerned about completing their tasks and were anxious to ask the questions that they had prepared in order to ensure that the **SLOs** were achieved. The students continued listening because they were aware of the importance of being courteous at all times. Eventually, Sharon decided to take the initiative and asked the HR manager if the group could ask the questions they had prepared. Some had already been dealt with during Evelyn's talk and so some students did not ask their designated questions. Nonetheless, they achieved many of the **S**pecific **L**earning **O**utcomes. The students also observed the application of health and safety regulations in the workplace and the importance placed on quality. The company had just received the ISO 9000 (an important international standard).

Some students recorded the main points in their templates, whilst others just listened. Craig thanked Evelyn Hernon for her time and also for answering all of their questions. At this point, Sharon mentioned that she was also presently doing a Career Investigation on the whole area of design. Evelyn, who had been extremely impressed with Sharon all during the visit, organised a short interview with their leading designer, who then offered Sharon a four-day work placement during her Easter holidays.

Sharon was thrilled with the visit because, not only had she gathered sufficient information for a Summary Report, but she had also covered her out-of-school learning experience for her Career Investigation, as well as having organised a work placement related to her career aspirations.

This visit was an extremely interesting experience and a great learning opportunity. Sharon benefited enormously from the visit because she participated actively all through it. She was aware of the connections between this experience and the other activities she was engaged in as part of the LCVP and she had the confidence to bring them up with the HR manager. As a result of her interest in the subject and her enthusiastic participation, she made a very good impression on the HR manager and gained a lot more from the experience than she had imagined she would. As with all LCVP activities, you should be actively involved in the learning cycle and not a passive onlooker.

POST-EXPERIENCE

RECORD
- Use templates.
- Use your LCVP folder.
- Write reports.
- Prepare a Recorded Interview/Presentation.

EVALUATE
1. **Debrief**: Reflect on the experience.
2. **Assess**
    (a) The activity
    (b) Personal performance
    (c) Group performance
    (d) Cross-curricular links
3. **Conclude and Recommend**
    (a) Draw conclusions.
    (b) Make recommendations based on your conclusions.
    (c) Suggest follow-on activities.

You have now reached the **P**ost-experience stage of this experience. You went through the **P**re-experience steps required to plan the experience. You have been through the activity stage of the process by participating in the activity itself and now, in the **P**ost-experience stage, you will be in a position to reflect on the experience and see if you have achieved the aims that you set yourself at the start. The **P**ost-experience stage of the process is every bit as demanding as the other two and there are several steps that you must follow if you are to make sure that you end this activity as strongly as you started it. The **P**ost-experience stage can be broken up into the following steps:

1. **Evaluate**
    (a) **Debrief**: As you can see in the diagram above, debriefing involves taking time to reflect on the experience. Think about what happened, what you did and what you learned.
    (b) **Assess**: Think back on the activity you participated in and ask yourself how you performed. Did everything go smoothly? Did you run into any problems? How did you handle them? Then, look at how the group performed and ask yourself if there was good teamwork. Did people pull together to get the tasks assigned to them done? Did members of the group help and encourage each other? What Leaving Certificate subjects were useful?
    (c) **Conclude and recommend**: Draw conclusions. Based on those conclusions, make recommendations. Suggest follow-on activities.
2. **Record**: Use the templates in this book to record key words that spring to mind when you look back on the activity. Return to these key words at a later stage and elaborate on them. Finally, write a report.

Evaluate

It is important to stress the need to evaluate every experience. Evaluation looks at the relevance, quality, value and usefulness of the activity. Effective evaluation enables successes to be celebrated, areas of difficulty pin-pointed and plans put in place to eliminate known weaknesses. Evaluation is part of the learning cycle and **PEP** for all LCVP activities and usually takes place at the end of an activity.

You're revisiting the experience, looking back to check how far the activity went in achieving its objectives.

Steps in the Evaluation Process

1. **Debrief**: Reflect on the activity.
    - What happened?
    - What did you do?
    - What did you **learn**?
    - Did you meet your **objectives**?
2. **Assess**: Examine and discuss the information.
    - What went **well**?
    - What did **not work well**?
    - How well did the group work together?
    - How **useful** was the activity?
    - What Leaving Certificate subjects were relevant to this activity? Consider, in particular, your **V**ocational **S**ubject **G**roupings.
3. **Conclude and Recommend**: Draw conclusions. Based on those conclusions, make recommendations.
    - How can you improve for future activities?
    - Can you think of any follow-on activities?

Evaluating should enhance and make sense of the activity. Set aside sufficient **time** for evaluating. Participating in an activity encourages learning.

Plan opportunities for several evaluations. The **S**pecific **L**earning **O**utcomes (**SLOs**) are worth exploring in evaluation sessions.

Evaluation Methods   **List one advantage**

TYPES	ADVANTAGES
★ Questionnaires	
★ Class Discussion	
★ Teachers' Opinions	
★ Written Reports	

Reasons to Evaluate

- ✪ Getting feedback is important.
- ✪ It determines if the activity was worthwhile.
- ✪ It helps you to prepare for future activities.
- ✪ It determines if you achieved your objectives.
- ✪ It helps you to deal with any issues that arose during the activity.

Tip: Always evaluate each activity.

Evaluation Methods

1. Questionnaires

- ⇒ They are easy to prepare.
- ⇒ They are easy to collate.
- ⇒ They are inexpensive to produce.
- ⇒ Replies are confidential.
- ⇒ People respond well to questionnaires.
- ⇒ Everybody is given the same questions.

Tip: Allow plenty of **time** for evaluation.

2. Class Discussion

- ⇒ There's no need to prepare, therefore it's quick.
- ⇒ Comments made can be elaborated on.
- ⇒ Students practise communication skills.
- ⇒ Discussions include all students.
- ⇒ It provides an opportunity to compare the activity under discussion with other activities.

3. Teachers' Opinions/Speakers' Opinions

- ⇒ They can give their opinions quickly.
- ⇒ No costs are involved.
- ⇒ Teachers and speakers are in a good position to judge.
- ⇒ They can comment on the students' individual contributions.
- ⇒ Teachers can highlight the differences between this activity and others.

4. Written Report

- ⇒ Students can give individual comments.
- ⇒ It's easy to see what the students have learned.
- ⇒ It provides an opportunity to practise IT skills.
- ⇒ It can be used for assessment, both for the portfolio and in the written paper.

Note: Evaluation is important for both the **portfolio** and the **written exam.**

Debriefing: Possible Template for Rough Work

Use key words to record your ideas. Revisit the template at a later stage and elaborate on what you have written. Include it in your LCVP folder.

LCVP ACTIVITIES	CONCLUSIONS		RECOMMENDA-TIONS	GROUP PERFORMANCE	YOUR PERFORMANCE
Activities	What worked well?	What did not work well?	Suggested changes for future activities	How did the group perform?	How did you perform?
'My Own Place' Investigation					
Visit In					
Visit Out					
Career Investigation					
Work Placement					
Enterprise Activity					

Cross-Curricular Links (Link the Learning)

There are wide-ranging opportunities to develop cross-curricular links. The principal Specific Learning Outcomes that refer to cross-curricular learning are:

- Link the activities to learning in relevant Leaving Certificate subjects.
- Use learning from relevant Leaving Certificate subjects to formulate questions about aspects of a local enterprise/community enterprise.
- Integrate information from a variety of sources including relevant Leaving Certificate subjects.

There are other Specific Learning Outcomes that, although they do not refer specifically to cross-curricular links, offer many opportunities to create links.

- **Health and Safety**: This is also important in Chemistry, Home Economics, Construction Studies and Engineering.
- **Teamwork**: Teamwork is also important in Chemistry when students are participating in experiments.
- **Economic Activities**: These are also studied in Economics, Business, and Geography.

The responsibility for cross-curricular learning is placed on you. When **planning** or **debriefing** at the end of an activity always ask the cross-curricular questions:

- What Leaving Certificate subjects were particularly useful to you in this activity? In particular, were your Vocational Subject Groupings (**VSGs**) useful?
- How were these subjects useful?

Links between your Vocational Subject Groupings

A link could be established between music and business by having a music related enterprise activity, possibly a concert, and inviting an entrepreneur who has set up a business associated with music.

Links between your Vocational Subject Groupings and other Leaving Certificate subjects

An example of a link between your **VSGs** and other Leaving Certificate subjects is letter writing. This is a skill that is practised in English and may also be used in Business and the Link Modules.

Links between subjects and the wider community

There are many possible links between subjects and the community. Work placements, Visits Out and Career Investigations all create connections between the community and the school.

Cross-Curricular Links: Possible Template for Rough Work

My **V**ocational **S**ubject **G**roupings (**VSGs**)

1.	2.

LCVP Activities	Details	I found these LC subjects useful	How were they useful?
Visit In			
Visit Out			
Enterprise Activity			
'My Own Place' Investigation			
Work Placement			
Career Investigation			
Recorded Interview/ Presentation			

Portfolio tip: As you participate in activities, document the cross-curricular learning.

Record

The final step in the **P**ost-experience stage of any experience is to record that experience. You can choose to do this by writing a report or filming a recorded interview or presentation. At this stage of the experience, you have gathered, evaluated and assessed all the information you need and it remains only to present that information in a clear and concise way. You should make good use of the templates in this book and your LCVP folder when preparing to present your experience of an activity.

WAYS TO RECORD AN LCVP EXPERIENCE
⋆ **Write a report.**
⋆ **Make a Recorded Interview/Presentation.**

Report Writing in the LCVP

Report writing is an important skill, which will be valuable to students and relevant in their future lives: in education, in employment, in enterprise and in the community. In the LCVP there are three reports:

1. **Summary Report** (Core Portfolio Item)
2. **Enterprise Report** (Optional Portfolio Item)
3. **'My Own Place' Report** (Optional Portfolio Item)

Summary Report

The Summary Report in the LCVP is a very clear, short and concise written document. The report is based on an **LCVP activity** and the **S**pecific **L**earning **O**utcomes (**SLOs**) provide you with many possibilities for writing a Summary Report.

Reports are usually written in the past tense.

The Recorded Interview/Presentation

Leaving Certificate
Examination Number: 100450

This is an optional item in the portfolio which allows you to submit a video recording of yourself either being interviewed or making a presentation. The Recorded Interview/Presentation must be related to one or more of the **S**pecific **L**earning **O**utcomes of the Link Modules. The aim of the interview/presentation is to show your knowledge and your ability to communicate clearly ideas and opinions developed in the LCVP.

PORTFOLIO ITEM: SUMMARY REPORT

The LCVP will present many opportunities to use a Summary Report to record learning and experiences.

Examples may include:

* A **Visit Out** to a training scheme, community enterprise, voluntary organisation or business enterprise
* A **Visit In** (a visitor) to the LCVP class
* A **team-building** activity
* An **Enterprise Activity** (provided you don't submit an Enterprise Report in the options)
* A '**My Own Place' Investigation** (provided you don't submit a 'My Own Place' Report in the options)

Things to keep in mind

* Compulsory: As part of your portfolio you must present a total of **six** items. A Summary Report is part of the **mandatory** core.
* Your Summary Report must be presented as a word-processed document (300–600 words long).
* Use a regular font such as Times New Roman, size 12pt.
* Use language that is simple, accurate and concise.
* Use short sentences and short paragraphs.
* The use of bold headings and bulleted lists is recommended.
* Your report may include tabulated information.
* Do not include appendices.

> **Core**
> Submit all 4
> **Optional**
> Submit 2 out of 4
> A total of **6 portfolio items** must be submitted.

Assessment Criteria – Syllabus

The Summary Report will assess your ability to:

* Generate a document with a clear and consistent layout.
* Name the LCVP activity being reported.
* State the terms of reference of the report or aims of the activity.
* Summarise key details of the activity under headings.
* Use language appropriate to the task content.
* Organise the report in a logical sequence.
* Draw conclusions and make recommendations appropriate to previously stated aims/terms of reference.

Summary Report: Guidelines for Report Structure

1. **Title**: Include a clear title, e.g. 'A summary report on an LCVP visit to Intel'.

2. **Author's name**, i.e. your name should also be included.

3. (a) **Terms of Reference**
    This explains why the report was written.
    Or

    (b) **Aims of the Activity**
    Explain what you/your class hoped to learn/achieve from the activity.

4. **Body of the Report**
    *   Summarise your main findings.
    *   Remember the learning cycle – **P**re-experience, **E**xperience, **P**ost-experience.
    *   Arrange information in a logical sequence under bold headings and bulleted lists.
    *   Write in chronological order or in order of importance.
    *   Don't forget to mention **your responsibilities**, i.e. your individual contribution.
    *   The report should have a clear **beginning, middle and end**.

5. **Conclusions**: Include a concise list of conclusions that you have come to as a result of the activity or investigation. Your conclusions should refer back to the original terms of reference or aims presented at the start of the report.

6. **Recommendations**: These are suggestions for future action based on your **conclusions**. They may also include ideas for follow-on activities or describe how you might perform better in a future activity.

7. **Appendices**: No appendices are required.

In the case of a group activity, the report must show your own individual contribution.

Summary Report: Possible Template for Rough Work

Title:
Author:
Aims
Body of Report
Conclusions
Recommendations

Portfolio Tip: Use this template to record key words. Revisit them later and elaborate on them in your LCVP folder. Begin to word-process and keep a copy to review and improve.

SAMPLE PORTFOLIO ITEM

SUMMARY REPORT

Title:
A Visit Out to Itleads Ltd as part of our LCVP

Author:
Alan Whitney

Aims
- To investigate a local enterprise as part of my LCVP Link Modules
- To learn about the management and operation of a call centre
- To establish if I would like a career in telesales

Prior to the Visit
We contacted Itleads and organised a date with permission from our principal. We brainstormed some questions and did some research on the company, using the Internet.

Research Findings
Itleads was founded in May 2004 to provide enterprise, prospecting and telemarketing services to technology companies worldwide. Itleads is a fast-growing company with a multi-lingual staff and offices in the US, Germany, the UK and Ireland.

Visit
Miss Mary Madden met us at reception and I introduced the group. We were given some background information about the company, who owned it and what it actually did. She also explained that their main market was Europe and that the Sligo office was their main base and expanding at an enormous rate.

The Call Centre
She then brought us to the call centre. Because this is a working office we had to be very quiet. There were 100 people, mainly females, working in one large office. Each employee had their own desk and a phone headset. That week, the employees were marketing business solutions software for Intel. Each employee has to meet daily, weekly and monthly targets. These targets are broken down as follows:

- 80 phone calls a day
- Generate 5 sales leads per week

Madden explained the following about the call centre:

employee uses a database which contains addresses, phone numbers and contact details for anies worldwide.
employee contacts these companies to determine whether they are interested in buying the which they are marketing.
n produce a detailed report which informs Intel of what companies are interested in ir product and when.

End of Tour
At the end of the tour we were given a folder, which contained stationery with Itleads' logo. We had an opportunity to ask questions and we thanked Miss Madden. On returning to school we debriefed that afternoon and wrote down our main points using a Summary Report template. I documented main points in my LCVP folder.

Conclusions
- I enjoyed my visit and felt that the majority of my aims were met.
- I learned about a local enterprise in my area and in particular one that dealt with technology and it was an interesting way to achieve a number of the **S**pecific **L**earning **O**utcomes of the LCVP.
- I observed how a call centre works and what it actually does.
- I came to the conclusion that I would not like a career in telesales. There were too many targets and too much pressure to make sales, as well as too much time spent on the phone.

Recommendations
I felt that the tour was too short. I would have liked to have interviewed one of the girls on the call centre floor to ask her questions about her job. I found it difficult to understand exactly what Itleads do. Since they mainly deal with technology companies, I wasn't familiar with the products that they were trying to sell, as it was business software. I'd recommend that we should have researched more about software packages. We should also have asked for some time to interview an employee as it was mostly listening and observing from a manager's point of view. However, I sourced a lot of information and would recommend a Visit Out as an interesting activity.

The Recorded Interview/Presentation

The NCCA guidelines recommend the following when preparing for a Recorded Interview/Presentation.

The student interviewee/presenter should:	The interviewer/s should:
• dress **neatly** and appropriately	• be familiar with the aims and expected outcomes of the Link Modules
• adopt an open, relaxed posture	• plan key questions to provide structure and direction to the interview
• make **eye contact** with interviewer/audience	• avoid complex or ambiguous questions (e.g. 'What subjects are you studying at school? Why did you choose them and which is your favourite?')
• **listen carefully** and affirm questions with appropriate body language	
• **speak clearly** and confidently using normal conversational voice	
• express **ideas/opinions/points** in a logical sequence	• articulate questions clearly
• take care not to drop voice at the end of sentences	• adapt questions to the level of student's abilities
• avoid reading from notes or from visual aids	• use open questions (e.g. 'Tell me about..., Why do you think...?'
• avoid distracting mannerisms, jargon, slang	• encourage students to give examples and express their opinions
• explain **technical terms** which may be unfamiliar to interviewer/audience	• give students time to think after they are questioned
• use **hand gestures** where appropriate	• follow up on student's responses
• use action words and phrases when describing events (e.g. I planned... we evaluated...)	• avoid dominating the interview
• make reference to **skills gained** through Link Module activities	

Note: A documentary style video recording in which you act as a narrator is not recommended, as it is unlikely to satisfy the assessment.

Remember, it's an LCVP Recorded Interview/Presentation and must relate to LCVP activities and demonstrate what you have learned.

PORTFOLIO ITEM: THE RECORDED INTERVIEW/PRESENTATION

Leaving Certificate
Examination Number: 100450

The Recorded Interview/Presentation must be related to one or more of the **S**pecific **L**earning **O**utcomes of the Link Modules. The aim of the interview/presentation is to show your knowledge and your ability to communicate clearly ideas and opinions developed in the LCVP.

The Recorded Interview/Presentation can take a variety of forms, for example:

★ A simulated job interview.
★ A general interview based on participation in and insights gained through the Link Modules.
★ A short presentation. This is then followed by 2–3 questions, based on content.

Things to keep in mind

★ Optional: As part of your portfolio, you must present a total of **six items**. The Recorded Interview/Presentation is part of the optional items.
★ The Recorded Interview/Presentation should last a minimum of **three minutes** and a maximum of **five minutes**.
★ Make sure that you research your questions and come up with relevant answers. Understand the **S**pecific **L**earning **O**utcomes and apply your own personal experiences.
★ Make sure there is variety of tone in your speaking voice.
★ Communicate your opinions clearly.
★ Be confident. Use gestures that suggest enthusiasm for your subject.
★ Ensure that you are neat and tidy in appearance.
★ Don't give short answers to questions. Go into detail. Expand and elaborate. For example, if, during an interview on your work placement, you are asked to discuss your work placement, you could cover the following subjects in your answer: the type of work; why you chose it; the experience gained; what you learned; the skills acquired and their relevance to the world of work; how you can apply what you learned at school/home and in the community; and what you think of the work placement as part of the Link Modules in the LCVP.

Assessment Criteria – Syllabus

The Recorded Interview/Presentation will assess your ability to:
★ Communicate effectively in appropriate depth and detail.
★ Express an informed opinion.
★ Support answers to questions with relevant examples.
★ Engage positively with the interviewer/audience.
★ Use appropriate body language.

Restrictions

The content of a Career Investigation, Summary Report or any other optional item submitted as part of your portfolio may not be the principal topic of your Recorded Interview/Presentation. As a general rule, an activity already submitted in your portfolio should not make up more than **25 per cent** of the Recorded Interview.

Interview

An interview is an opportunity to show your talents. As part of your portfolio, you can submit a 3–5 minute Recorded Interview on video. There are two main options for this interview: you can choose to do a simulated job interview or you can do a general interview of your experiences in the LCVP. This general interview could be seen as a summing-up of your whole LCVP experience.

Recorded Interview

Pre-interview

- Watch previous LCVP interviews.
- Research and prepare questions. Practise answers.
- Be aware of the **SLOs** and have examples of how you achieved them ready.
- Make sure that the questions you are asked give you a chance to talk about your strengths.
- Be aware of the **Assessment Criteria**.
- Be aware of the **NCCA Guidelines**, see p. 23.
- Be aware of the **Marking Scheme**, see p. 221.
- Make sure that the interviewer has your questions and that, if he/she is not your teacher, that he/she is familiar with the LCVP Link Modules.

During the Interview

- Make sure that the location is suitable, i.e. you'll need a quiet room with suitable lighting. Make sure the school bell is switched off.
- Communicate positively and confidently.
- Maintain eye contact with the camera at all times.
- Use positive body language: don't slouch or fold your arms; try to appear open and relaxed; smile!
- Make sure that you are dressed neatly and appropriately.
- The recording must be at least **three** minutes and no more than **five** minutes long.
- Start recording only after you have sat down.
- Display your **Leaving Certificate Examination number at all times.**
- Place the camera on a tripod and use an external microphone.

Students preparing for
interviews through role-play.

Post-interview

- Watch your performance.
- Check that your exam number can be seen.
- See if there is anything you can improve on.
- Check if there are any additional points you would like to make in the interview.
- Go through the scoring sheet (see p. 29) and the Assessment Criteria.

Note: Be aware of non-verbal communication. This is communicating through body language and tone of voice. Sometimes **how you say** something is more important than **what you say**.

General Interview: Possible Template for Rough Work

1. Tell me about yourself.

2. What do you hope to do after the Leaving Certificate?

3. Tell me about your work experience during the LCVP.

Prepare answers to these questions. Elaborate, express opinions and give LCVP examples where appropriate. Remember, practice makes the perfect Recorded Interview/Presentation.

4. What are the main differences between work and school?

5. How will the LCVP help you in third level or work?

Make sure that your recording presents a variety of activities you participated in during the LCVP.

6. When, in the LCVP, did you work in a team and what did you learn about teams?

7. What do you understand by enterprise?

8. Tell me about any other activities you participated in during the LCVP.

A general interview must be based on participation and insights gained through the Link Modules.

★ The success of an interview depends on the types of questions asked.
★ You may decide to develop your own questions.
★ Role-play with the above interview questions.
★ Use score sheets.
★ Ask yourself how you can improve.

Examples of topics for the presentation may include:
- 'My Own Place' investigation
- Job-seeking skills – how to prepare for an interview
- How to conduct a meeting
- Teamwork
- Voluntary/community organisations
- Idea generation
- Promotional video, e.g. 'An Introduction to the LCVP'

Tip: Your presentation should last 3–5 minutes. You must include 2–3 questions based on the content of the presentation.

Note: Make sure the presentation is related to the **S**pecific **L**earning **O**utcomes of the LCVP.

PRESENTATION

Plan
Relax
Elaborate
Structure
Effective
Neat
Tone
Assessment
Trial Run
Interesting
Original
Number Displayed

Note: Make sure you display your exam number at all times during the presentation.

PROPER PRIOR PLANNING PREVENTS POOR PERFORMANCE

- Know the room.
- Know your material.
- Learn how to relax.
- Concentrate on your presentation.
- Gain experience.

Presentation: Guidelines for Structure

A presentation is a form of communication. Make sure that it will be remembered and understood. The following guidelines may help you to develop good presentation skills.

1. **Plan** your presentation. At least one hour's planning is recommended for each minute of a 5-minute presentation.

2. Formulate your **objectives**.
    * List and prioritise your top three goals.
    * What do you want to accomplish?
    * Keep it short and simple.

3. **Structure** your presentation. Remember it is an **LCVP presentation**. It should have a recognisable opening, middle and end.
    * **Opening** (5–10% of time): Arouse attention. Establish a theme.
    * **Middle** (80% of time): Introduce sub-topics, offer detail and elaborate.
    * **End** (5-10% of time): Make a strong final impression.
      Lastly, make sure that you are asked 2–3 questions on the content of the presentation.

4. **Delivery**: When presenting be aware of the following:
    * **Eyes**: Maintain eye contact. It can be very effective.
    * **Voice**: Speak a little more loudly and slightly more slowly than you normally do. Watch the news on TV to get the hang of this. You must project your voice and vary the tone.
    * **Expression**: Remember you can enhance what you say with your facial expressions. Don't forget to smile.
    * **Appearance**: Wear your proper uniform and make sure that you are clean and neat. Don't forget your tie!
    * **Posture**: Look relaxed without looking casual. Stand comfortably in front of the camera. Be aware of your body language.

This structure is also useful for Recorded Interviews.

5. **Visual aids**: These can be used and can enhance your presentation by adding variety and authenticity. They can also leave a lasting impression. Examples include sketches, maps, graphs, posters, pictures, products, overhead projector, PowerPoint etc. Make sure that the **visual aids** supplement the speech rather than becoming the speech itself. They should be relevant and pleasing to the eye. Make sure you practise your presentation using your visual aids, so that you are comfortable holding them, pointing to them etc.

RECORDED INTERVIEW/PRESENTATION

A practice score sheet:

	Rating (1-10)	Comment
Clarity of Voice and Thought		
Fluency		
Eye Contact		
Gestures		
Humour		
Structure (logical sequence)		
Voice		
Appearance		
Posture		
Are answers detailed enough?		
Links to SLOs		
Pace: Are you speaking too fast?		
Content		
Confidence		
Informed Opinions		
Personal Examples		
Wrap-Up		
Variety of Tone		
Overall Rating	/180	

Tip: Ask your teacher or your friend to rate your Recorded Interview/ Presentation.

CONCLUSION: APPLYING PEP TO LCVP ACTIVITIES

The three stages of **PEP** – **P**re-experience, **E**xperience and **P**ost-experience – can and should be applied to every activity you undertake during the LCVP. Whether you are doing a work placement, visiting a local voluntary organisation or conducting a Career Investigation, your success will depend on a serious, step-by-step approach to the experience, which takes account of the valuable work you need to do before, during and after it.

This section has guided you step by step through the processes involved in planning, experiencing and evaluating an activity. Now, we will go through all three stages of this learning process with two popular LCVP activities: Visits In and Visits Out.

Visitors/Visit In

Inviting visitors to the classroom can be an extremely interesting experience and a great learning opportunity. As with all LCVP activities, inviting a visitor to speak requires that you are actively involved in the learning cycle and not a passive onlooker. A visitor to the classroom is an excellent way of generating interest in a certain topic or area and is something you should really do.

Reasons for Inviting a Visitor

- A Visit In is part of the LCVP syllabus **S**pecific **L**earning **O**utcomes (**SLOs**). You are encouraged to arrange a visitor from a training scheme, community enterprises, voluntary organisations and/or a business enterprise.
- You can base a portfolio item on such a visit, for example:
    - An Enterprise/Action Plan
    - A Summary Report
- A Visit In can make you more aware of your area and/or local organisations.
- A Visit In will provide you with information.
- It is good public relations (PR) for the school.
- You might establish contacts for a work placement or for an interview for your Career Investigation.

> **Portfolio Tip:** Use a **Summary Report** template and record information in your **LCVP folder**.

Who can you invite?

- Teaching staff
- Former students (preferably a former LCVP student)
- Parents/family/friends
- City and County Enterprise Boards
- Health Boards
- Planning Authorities
- Local enterprises
- Voluntary and community organisations
- Financial institutions, e.g. banks, credit unions
- Others

VISITOR
Cornelia Sa[...]

Planning a Visit In

The **Enterprise/Action Plan** template (see p. 7) is ideal for **planning** this activity. Look particularly at aims/objectives and research and ask yourself the following questions:

1. What does the visitor need to know about us?
2. What do we need to know about the visitor?
3. How will the visit be organised?
4. What do we hope to learn from the visitor?
5. When and how will we evaluate and record the learning?

> **Portfolio tip:** Use the **Enterprise/Action Plan** template when planning a Visit In.

Pre-visit

- Research the speaker and organisation and hold a class discussion about the proposed visit.
- Brainstorm a list of questions using the **S**pecific **L**earning **O**utcomes. Don't waste time asking questions if you have already researched the information.
- Ensure that your objectives are **SMART**: **S**pecific, **M**easurable, **A**ttainable and **R**ealistic in the **T**ime frame.
- Assign different responsibilities to each student, e.g. meeting the visitor, introducing the visitor, asking questions, thanking the visitor etc.
- Arrange the room to suit the activity. Place a notice on the door and make sure the intercom is switched off. Organise suitable equipment, e.g. overhead/video/data projector.
- Distribute name tags, photocopies of questions, templates etc.
- Arrange for the use of a camera/camcorder, but make sure you get permission to film from the visitor.

During the Visit

- Be courteous at all times.
- Make sure that everybody has a copy of the plan for the activity, so that you can easily check who is supposed to be doing each task and when, e.g. which students are responsible for providing water and glasses?
- Listen attentively to the visitor.
- Record main points, perhaps using a report template.
- Ask any questions that you prepared in advance.
- Complete the tasks assigned to you.
- Thank the visitor.

> **Tip:** Speakers should speak for **5-10 minutes** and answer questions for the next 15 minutes. Use the remaining class time to **evaluate**.

Post-visit

- Did the visit go according to plan?
- What worked well?
- How did you engage as a team?
- What would you do differently?
- Did each student participate?
- Did anything go wrong? Why?
- Did you have an individual role?
- Send a thank-you message, by letter, e-mail or telephone.
- Write a Summary Report on the visit.

> **Tip:** How many SLOs did we achieve?

Visit In – A Checklist to facilitate a Visit In

★ Is our room suitable? ❏

★ Do we have an overhead projector/video/DVD data projector? ❏

★ Do we have water/jug/glasses? ❏

★ Do we have a 'Do not Disturb' sign for the door? ❏

★ Has the intercom been switched off? ❏

★ Have questions been photocopied? ❏

★ Have all students been informed to bring pen and paper/template? ❏

★ Has a student been organised to meet the visitor at the office? ❏

★ Has the principal been informed and is he/she available? ❏

★ Is a camcorder/camera available? ❏

★ Has the speaker agreed to the use of a camcorder/camera? ❏

★ Has the speaker been briefed on the LCVP and questions? ❏

★ Has a student been nominated to introduce the visitor? ❏

★ Has each student been assigned to ask a question? ❏

★ Have students been assigned to ask additional questions to avoid awkward silences? ❏

★ Has a student been assigned to thank the visitor and conclude the talk? ❏

★ Has a student been assigned to thank the speaker, by letter, in a telephone call or by e-mail? ❏

★ Have evaluation sheets been organised? ❏

Any additional comments, e.g. a possible **follow-on activity**, perhaps a **fund-raiser**:_____

_____

Summary Report: Possible Template for Rough Work

Tip: Use this Summary Report template to record the main points. Revisit and elaborate on them and then document them in your LCVP folder.

VISIT IN SUMMARY REPORT

Title:	**Actual Visit** (Questions asked, what you learned)
Author:	
Terms of Reference (Why was the report written?)	
Aims (What do you hope to achieve from the activity?)	**My Thoughts**
Introduction (Reason for the Visit In)	**Conclusions** (Link back to aims/terms of reference)
Planning	
Research	**Recommendations** (follow-on activities)
Visitor (Name, organisation, date)	

Visit Out (Visit to an Enterprise and/or Voluntary Organisation)

Tip: Use an Enterprise/Action Plan template to plan your Visit Out.

Visiting an enterprise and/or a voluntary organisation can be an extremely interesting experience and a great learning opportunity. As with all LCVP activities, visiting an organisation requires that you are actively involved in the learning cycle and not passive onlookers. To obtain the maximum benefit from the visit you need maximum preparation.

Pre-visit

- ✿ Decide on a business/organisation and gather as much information as possible about it, e.g. search websites, e-mail them, telephone or write a letter.
- ✿ Obtain permission for the visit from the school principal.
- ✿ Contact the business/organisation giving your name, school, teacher, times, dates and number of students.
- ✿ Agree on a date and time and make travel arrangements. Ensure all pupils are covered by insurance.
- ✿ If there are costs involved, collect money from all students.
- ✿ Brainstorm a list of questions to ask during the visit.
- ✿ Hold a class discussion about the proposed visit and the different tasks each student has, e.g. one person to introduce the group and one person to thank the business/organisation.
- ✿ Inform your other teachers, giving them the date and time.

During the visit

- ✿ Be courteous at all times.
- ✿ Make sure that everybody has a copy of the plan for the activity, so that you can easily check who is supposed to be doing each task and when, e.g. which students are responsible for making sure that everybody is on the bus.
- ✿ Listen attentively during the visit and ask relevant questions.
- ✿ Record main points and observations, perhaps using a template of a report.
- ✿ Complete tasks assigned.
- ✿ Observe rules and regulations, e.g. health and safety regulations in the workplace.

Fire
✓ assembly
point

Post-visit

- ✿ Hold a class discussion about all aspects of the visit.
- ✿ Did the visit go according to plan?
- ✿ Did anything go wrong? Why?
- ✿ What worked well?
- ✿ Did each student participate?
- ✿ Discuss different ways to evaluate the visit and then evaluate.
- ✿ Send a thank-you message by letter, e-mail or telephone.
- ✿ Write a Summary Report on the visit.

Tip: How many SLOs did we achieve?

Visit Out – A Checklist to facilitate a Visit Out

★ Has the school principal been asked for permission to do this? ☐

★ What is the time, date and duration of the visit? ☐

★ What is the name and phone number of your contact at the organisation you're visiting? ☐

★ Has transport been organised? Do you need a map? ☐

★ Have consent forms been sent to parents and returned? ☐

★ Have insurance forms been organised? ☐

★ Have questions been prepared? ☐

★ Has the organisation been informed? ☐

★ Do you have the school phone number in case of an emergency? ☐

★ Has everybody got a notebook/template and pen? ☐

★ Have we arranged a person to introduce the group? ☐

★ Do we need a camera/camcorder? ☐

★ Has the business/organisation granted permission to film? ☐

★ Has each student been briefed on the tasks? ☐

★ Has a student been assigned to thank your contact at the end of your visit ? ☐

★ Has a student been assigned to thank the organisation, by letter, by telephone, or by e-mail? ☐

Any additional comments, e.g. a possible **follow-on activity**, perhaps a **fund-raiser**:_____

_____

Each student should make an individual contribution to the activity.

You could draw up a set of rules for a Visit Out. You could also divide rules into Pre-visit, Visit and Post-visit. Document the rules in your LCVP folder; remember this may be a question in the written examination.

Summary Report: Possible Template for Rough Work

Tip: Use this Summary Report template to record the main points. Revisit and elaborate on them and then document them in your LCVP folder.

VISIT OUT SUMMARY REPORT

Title:

Author:

Terms of Reference
(Why was the report written?)

Aims
(What do you hope to achieve from the activity?)

Introduction
(Reason for the Visit Out)

Planning

Research

Visitor
(Name, organisation, date)

Actual Visit
(Questions asked, what you learned)

My Thoughts

Conclusions
(Link back to aims/terms of reference)

Recommendations
(follow-on activities)

LINK MODULE 1 – PREPARATION FOR THE WORLD OF WORK

UNIT 1 – INTRODUCTION TO WORKING LIFE

The aim of this unit is to encourage you to find out for yourself as much as possible about **working life** and **local employment opportunities**. The term 'working life' is used here in the broadest sense and includes paid employment and unpaid voluntary work. Many of the **S**pecific **L**earning **O**utcomes of this unit may be achieved by engaging in a local study of 'My Own Place'. This unit should be integrated with Units 2 and 3 of the Enterprise Education Link Module.

SPECIFIC LEARNING OUTCOMES – SLOs

(as listed in the syllabus)

When you have finished working through this unit, you should be able to:

1.1   identify the main sources of employment in the local area
1.2   identify the main social services and job creation agencies in the local area
1.3   identify the main agencies that provide transport in the local area
1.4   identify the main financial institutions servicing the needs of the local area
1.5   identify the main agencies involved in industrial relations in the local area
1.6   identify the principal economic activities in the local area
1.7   evaluate the potential for tourism in the local area
1.8   identify and understand the main differences between school and work
1.9   describe the intrinsic value of various forms of work, including self-employment and voluntary work
1.10 understand current regulations/legislation relating to the employment of young workers
1.11 understand current Health and Safety regulations in workplaces
1.12 role-play a situation that could give rise to a dispute in the workplace
1.13 understand issues related to diversity in the workplace
1.14 list the different forms of assistance for unemployed people
1.15 arrange a visit to a training scheme in the locality and/or invite an appropriate speaker from such an organisation to visit the group in the school
1.16 link the activities in this unit to learning in relevant Leaving Certificate subjects

'MY OWN PLACE'

An investigation of 'My Own Place' is an investigation into certain aspects of the local area, such as employment, transport, financial institutions, tourism, community and business enterprises and voluntary organisations. It creates an awareness of local employment and services.

Many of the **S**pecific **L**earning **O**utcomes in Unit 1 can be achieved through a 'My Own Place' investigation. A 'My Own Place' investigation offers a huge range of learning experiences and can benefit you when answering the written paper, i.e. the general questions, the audio-visual section and the Case Study. The Case Study may be an overview of a local issue. In compiling your **portfolio** you may decide to submit an Enterprise/Action Plan, a Summary Report or a 'My Own Place' Report. It's also beneficial for the Recorded Interview/Presentation.

A 'My Own Place' investigation is an ideal opportunity to develop **team** skills. It's interesting that sometimes we know very little about our local area. In this investigation, the diversity of subject matter and the limited time available to you means that you need to have clear objectives. Ensure your objectives are **SMART**: **S**pecific, **M**easurable, **A**chievable and **R**ealistic in the **T**ime frame.

Try and achieve a number of **S**pecific **L**earning **O**utcomes, as well as ensuring adequate information for the assessment.

Definition of 'My Own Place'

'My Own Place' has **a broad definition** to cater for both urban and rural settings. It can include the following:

- Class survey to decide on 'My Own Place'
- My route to school (walk, bike, car, bus, Luas, Dart, train)
- Street survey
- A suitable local shopping centre, industrial estate, block of shops to survey
- My local village/town

Pupils take different routes to school.

Possible topics for investigation can be divided up as follows:

Preparation for the World of Work – Link Module 1
- Identify the main sources of employment in the local area
- Social services
- Job creation agencies
- Transport
- Financial institutions
- Industrial relations
- Principal economic activities
- Potential for tourism

Tip: Use these headings and devise a questionnaire.

Note: This unit is integrated with Units 2 and 3 of the Enterprise Education Link Module.

Enterprise Education – Link Module 2
- A range of business enterprises
- Local community enterprises
- Local voluntary organisations

'My Own Place' is quite extensive and may be best achieved by engaging in a **number of investigations** whilst doing other activities. Use a team approach to generate all the Specific Learning Outcomes. The templates and writing frames will prompt you with ideas. If you decide to submit a 'My Own Place' Report, make sure that it meets the assessment criteria.

Tips for Writing about 'My Own Place'

- Decide on **objectives**. Make them **SMART**: **S**pecific, **M**easurable, **A**ttainable and **R**ealistic and give each a Time frame.
- Define the area and the **scope** of the investigation.
- Sketch a **map**.
- **Research** 'My Own Place' using a variety of methods: questionnaires, interviews, the Internet, etc.
- What **S**pecific **L**earning **O**utcomes (SLOs) can you achieve?
- Use a **team** approach and divide work.
- **Brainstorm** possible questions.
- Invite a **speaker**, e.g. someone who works in planning.
- Do a **SWOT** analysis (**S**trengths, **W**eaknesses, **O**pportunities and **T**hreats).
- Investigate at least one voluntary organisation, community enterprise and business enterprise in detail.
- Arrange a walking tour, if possible and/or a **Visit Out/Visit In.**

Tip: Use an Enterprise/Action Plan template to plan 'My Own Place'.

Remember the report on 'My Own Place' may be based on a single investigation over a short period or on a number of events, which take place at intervals over the two years of the Link Modules.

Since the 'My Own Place' Report involves assessing a number of skills and information, you may decide to write this detailed report after participating in all of the LCVP activities. Activities such as teamwork, researching and investigating will help you to prepare this detailed report. Use an Enterprise/Action Plan template to plan this investigation, which ensures a **portfolio item.**

Useful Resources...
- Local newspapers
- Local directories
- Golden Pages
- Internet
- Fáilte Ireland
- Citizen Information Centre
- Planning Office
- City and County Enterprise Boards
- Chamber of Commerce
- Library
- County Council
- Subject Teachers
- Others

Kildare County Enterprise Board

NEWBRIDGE NEWS

'MY OWN PLACE'

Define 'My Own Place'	Draft a map/sketch

An Art student may design a map.

Choose a definition that will suit the class, e.g. a local industrial estate.

Designed by Fiona Mc Ardle.

List possible visitors	A brief history of 'My Own Place'

Ask History students in your class for help.

Events in 'My Own Place'	Newspaper clippings

Take photos	Issues in 'My Own Place'

Ideas: lack of facilities, litter.

Aspects that can be investigated	Brainstorming ideas

Tip: Use the related Specific Learning Outcomes, e.g. tourism.

A Writing Frame to Generate Information on 'My Own Place'

Getting Started

The **best** aspect about 'My Own Place' is...

The aspects that need to be **improved** in 'My Own Place' are...

The main source of **employment** in 'My Own Place' is...

The main **social services** are *hospitals, clinics, Information Centres...*

The main **job creation agencies** are *FÁS...*

The main agencies that provide **transport** are *buses, trains, taxis, airports...*

The main **financial institutions** are *banks, building societies, insurance companies and credit unions...*

The main agencies involved in **industrial relations** are *ICTU, SIPTU, IMPACT...*

The principal **economic activities** are *primary, secondary, tertiary services...*

There is potential for tourism in 'My Own Place'...

Tip: Use a team approach to obtain information.

The local enterprises are:

Name	Product/Service	Markets	Employees
A.			
B.			
C.			
D.			
List Others			

Note: The information sourced using this template will help you to prepare for the written exam.

The main **community enterprises** are *LEADER groups, FÁS…*

The main **voluntary organisations** are *Amnesty International, the GAA, the St Vincent de Paul…*

The main **business/enterprise supports** are *City & County Enterprise Boards…*

The main **training agencies** are *FÁS, VTOS…*

Local Authorities in 'My Own Place' are…

INTRODUCTION TO WORKING LIFE

- **Work** can be defined as an activity which requires effort, e.g. washing the dishes at home.
- **Employment** is when payment is received for working, e.g. washing dishes in a canteen and getting paid. People in employment are employers, employees or self-employed.
- **Employers** are people who hire workers in return for payment.
- **Employees** are people who work for employers.
- **Self-employed** people work for themselves.

School To Work

When leaving school to start your working life, you will face a lot of **challenges**:
- Time management
- Money management
- New relationships and different roles
- Rights
- Responsibilities
- Freedom and independence
- Others

> What are the main differences between work and school?

Note: It is important to be aware of **local employment opportunities** and services.

Different types of work

Employment

Self-employment

Charity Work

WORK

Voluntary Work

Homework

Housework

> How many types of work are you involved in?

Voluntary Work

Many voluntary organisations rely on people to work for nothing and help the less well-off, e.g. the St Vincent de Paul. Voluntary work is very important to our society. If you have the opportunity to do voluntary work, you will see that it offers many benefits: you can help others, improve your self-esteem and acquire new skills.

Samantha Mumba is a special representative for Unicef Ireland.

Self-Employment

This is when you work for yourself, e.g. butchers, shop owners, builders and hairdressers.

ADVANTAGES	DISADVANTAGES
○ You're the boss. ○ You keep all the profits after tax. ○ You can develop a hobby. ○ It's an alternative to unemployment. ○ You decide your working hours. ○ You make the decisions.	○ You have to work long hours initially. ○ You alone are responsible for the business. ○ No one shares any losses with you. ○ There is a risk of failure. ○ You have limited finance.

Can you name any self-employed people in your area?

Would you consider self-employment?

Employment

When you commence employment, you may have a full-time or part-time position, or you may be employed on a contract basis. As an employee, you may have the opportunity to **job-share** or work **flexitime**. In return for working, you will receive remuneration or payment of some kind. The main form of remuneration is **wages**, which can be paid on the basis of hours worked (**time-rate**), units produced (**piece-rate**), percentage of sales (**commission**) or a fixed monthly **salary**. You may also receive an additional bonus or a percentage of profits (**profit-sharing**). In addition to wages or salaries, you may receive rewards called **benefits-in-kind**, e.g. a company car or VHI/BUPA payments. There are also non-financial benefits associated with employment, e.g. self-esteem.

Permanent Full-Time

If you are fortunate enough to have a permanent job, there are many advantages and disadvantages. They are outlined in the box below.

ADVANTAGES	DISADVANTAGES
○ You will have a regular income. ○ You do not have to worry about finding a job. ○ You can join a pension scheme. ○ It is easier to plan your own finances and future. ○ Security of employment gives independence. ○ Promotion prospects exist. ○ You are less likely to become depressed.	○ You have no incentive to move job. ○ Work tends to be less varied. ○ Less leisure/family time is available. ○ You may lose flexibility. ○ Moving house becomes more difficult. ○ Motivation may decrease.

Part-Time Work

With part-time work, you work a minimum of eight hours a week on a **regula**r basis.

Time-Rate

If an employee is paid by time-rate, his/her hours must be monitored.

How can time-keeping be monitored?

1. Sign in an attendance book
2. Clock in/clock out cards
3. Personal checks
4. Video cameras
5. Scan in ID cards

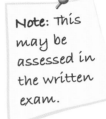

Note: This may be assessed in the written exam.

Why monitor?

1. Workers will learn to be punctual.
2. Wages can be calculated accurately.
3. One can check if employees are reliable.
4. Checks are a must for flexitime as employees will have a range of starting times.

Contract of Employment

When you are working, you must receive a **contract of employment**. This document sets out all the terms and conditions relating to the position offered.

A contract of employment will contain the following information:

- ✿ Employer's name and address
- ✿ Employee's name and address
- ✿ Job title
- ✿ Job description
- ✿ Date of commencement
- ✿ Salary
- ✿ Holiday entitlements
- ✿ Duration of contract/probationary period, if any
- ✿ Signature of employee
- ✿ Any other conditions of the job (hours of work/location)
- ✿ Pension arrangements

Note: This may be a written exam question.

Individuals may change their positions at work to move up, e.g. moving from an assistant manager to a manager.

What kind of conditions would my ideal job have?

_____

_____

Ideas!
- ✿ Hours of Work
- ✿ Wages
- ✿ Conditions
- ✿ Promotion
- ✿ Prospects

UNEMPLOYMENT

Many people are unable to find suitable employment and are said to be unemployed. This may happen due to the closure of businesses, a change in the economy or improvements in technology. When a person is unemployed, they receive unemployment benefit.

If you are unemployed for a time, you should look on this as an opportunity to develop new skills. **FÁS** offers fantastic training schemes for the unemployed.

Training Schemes for the Unemployed

What training courses are available for the unemployed?

- **FÁS**

  FÁS runs a large number of training courses, where you will receive a weekly training allowance. Depending on your circumstances, you may also receive travel, lunch and accommodation expenses.

- **Community Enterprise Scheme (CES)**

  This is for the long-term unemployed. Advice and training is given to a community-based group that has a viable plan to create local employment. This is an opportunity to enter part-time employment and work in local organisations so that the local area benefits.

- **Fáilte Ireland**

  As the National Tourism Development Authority, Fáilte Ireland provides opportunities for people over the age of 17, including the unemployed, to train for employment in the Irish tourist industry. Training is free and uniforms, lunch and a training allowance are provided for the three month duration of the FETAC accredited programmes.

- **VTOS Courses (Vocational Training Opportunities Scheme)**

  These are run by the Department of Education and Science and operated through the Vocational Education Committee (VECs). Unemployed adults are given the chance to learn new skills and prepare for work opportunities. They cover a wide range of subjects which can lead to qualifications such as the Junior Certificate, the Leaving Certificate, the Post-Leaving Certificate and City and Guilds Certificates.

FÁS Employment Services

FÁS is the National Training and Development Authority. It provides training for job-seekers, helps the unemployed to return to work and provides recruitment services. In particular, FÁS provides the following services:

- Initial guidance interviews to help build up your profile
- Career information including guidance, planning and support
- Advice on employment incentives, e.g. assistance for a person with disabilities
- Information on FÁS programmes and training
- Access to a wide range of job vacancy information
- They can submit your details to employers with suitable vacancies.

FÁS Employment Services give information on jobs in both Ireland and the rest of Europe. FÁS offices have touch screen computers on which job-seekers can search through current vacancies. This facility can also be accessed from home through the FÁS website. One of the packages offered on the touch screen computers is **Career Directions**.

Financial Assistance Available to the Unemployed

- ✿ Unemployment Benefit
- ✿ Family Income Supplement
- ✿ Back to Work Allowance
- ✿ Back to Work Enterprise Allowance
- ✿ Back to Education Allowance

Current rates and further information may be obtained from the Department of Social and Family Affairs, **www.welfare.ie.**

THE FUTURE OF WORK

The future of work is difficult to predict, with lots of changes possible as a result of globalisation, competition, changes in technology and also in our economies. Employees will need to be flexible and adaptable. Meeting the ever-changing demands of the workplace will be a lifelong challenge.

> A job for life is a thing of the past and careers for life are the exception rather than the rule.

Changes in Employment

- ✿ Employees change jobs and careers many times during their working life.
- ✿ More people work from home.
- ✿ Changes in technology mean the types of jobs available are changing continuously.
- ✿ More people are working part-time, job-sharing and working flexitime.
- ✿ More people are opting for self-employment.
- ✿ More people are working in services and trades.
- ✿ There are changes in economic activities.

Economic Activities describes the different types of businesses that exist. These can be divided into three categories:

1. Primary – agriculture, fishing, forestry and mining
2. Secondary – manufacturing and construction
3. Tertiary (Services) – financial, transport, legal and medical

> **Note:** You must be aware of **Economic Activities** in your 'My Own Place' invesigation.

RIGHTS AND RESPONSIBILITIES

Both employers and employees have rights and responsibilities.

Employees

As an employee/worker you have rights and responsibilities.

Employees' Rights

Redundancy

Written Contract of Employment

Maternity Leave

Safe & Healthy Working Place

Minimum Notice to Terminate Contract

Employees' Rights

Right to Join a Trade Union

Protection against Unfair Dismissal

Equal Pay

Holidays

No Discrimination

Employees' Responsibilities

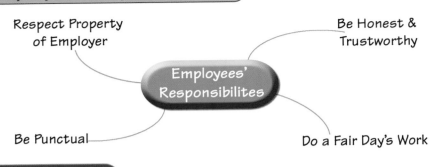

Respect Property
of Employer

Be Honest &
Trustworthy

Employees' Responsibilites

Be Punctual

Do a Fair Day's Work

Employers

Employers also have a range of rights and responsibilities.

Employers' Rights

To Run a Business

Hire Suitable
Staff

Employers' Rights

Dismiss Employees
Provided it's Fair

What is the minimum wage?

Employers' Responsibilities

Provide a
Written Contract

Pay Minimum Wage

Obey Laws

Employers' Responsibilites

No Discrimination

Proper Records,
e.g. PAYE & PRSI

Holidays

Safe & Healthy Workplace

THE LAW AND THE WORKPLACE

Health & Safety Regulations in the Workplace

Safety, Health and Welfare at Work Act 1993

The Health and Safety Authority is responsible for enforcing the Safety, Health and Welfare at Work Act 1993.

The Health and Safety Authority, a State-sponsored body, also promotes good standards, advice, research and information on health and safety in the workplace. It is responsible for developing and promoting new laws and standards. It inspects workplaces and investigates any accidents.

Safety, health and welfare are the responsibility of **both** the employer and the employee.

Think ... you may spend up to 50 years working, therefore it is important to have a safe and healthy workplace.

Employers' Obligations

- Employers must provide safe working conditions for all employees: safety signs should be clearly visible, a Safety Officer should be appointed and appropriate breaks for staff arranged.
- They should prepare a Safety Statement outlining hazards and how they can be overcome, eliminated or reduced.
- They should provide safe and protective clothing, footwear and equipment as required, e.g. providing safe computer monitors in offices and hard hats on construction sites.
- They should provide safety training, information and instructions where necessary and make employees aware of dangers, e.g. teach employees the safety procedures for using certain machines and what to do in the event of a fire.
- Employers should have an anti-bullying policy.
- They should facilitate the appointment of an employee as a Health and Safety Representative.

Employees' Responsibilities

- Employees should take responsibility for their own health, safety and welfare.
- They should use Personal Protective Equipment (PPE) and protective clothing, if required.
- They should follow training and instructions carefully.
- They should report any dangers or injuries to the Health and Safety Representative or employer.
- Employees should ensure there is no bullying in the workplace.

EMPLOYEES MUST REPORT ANY HAZARDS!

Safety Statement – This is a written document that identifies hazards, assesses risks and makes changes to ensure the workplace is safe. A Safety Statement is required by law. The statement is a declaration in writing of an employer's commitment to health and safety and it outlines how to achieve and maintain these standards.

All construction workers must have a **Safe Pass**; this is a one-day course organised by FÁS. Everyone on a construction site must have a Safe Pass. If you wish to participate in a work placement on a construction site, you must have a Safe Pass.

Note: Since March 2004, smoking in the workplace has been banned.

You must understand current health and safety regulations in the workplace and be able to follow a set of instructions relating to health and safety.

The objective of the legislation is to prevent accidents and ill health in the workplace. Remember, employers must carry out a hazard list and once these hazards have been identified, they must state what precautions have been taken and erect warning signs. Safety should be everyone's concern: employers', employees', visitors' etc.

Causes of Accidents in the Workplace

- ☼ Lack of training
- ☼ Untidy/cluttered areas
- ☼ Not following safety procedures
- ☼ Not wearing protective clothing
- ☼ Lack of concentration
- ☼ Not using machinery correctly
- ☼ Haste
- ☼ Horseplay

Complete a Health and Safety Audit of hazards in your school.

HAZARDS	WHAT SHOULD BE DONE TO ELIMINATE THESE HAZARDS?

DANGER
Toxic Hazard

Diversity in the Workplace

The workforce in Ireland has changed dramatically and now includes workers of all ages, races and religions and people with disabilities. The equality legislation in Ireland is not only concerned with gender equality. **The Employment Equality Act 1998–2004** outlines and outlaws discrimination on nine grounds:

Discrimination is when one person is treated less favourably than another.

1. Age
2. Gender
3. Marital status
4. Family status
5. Religion
6. Race
7. Sexual orientation
8. Membership of the traveller community
9. Disability

It's against the law to discriminate in the following areas:

- ☼ Recruitment
- ☼ Training
- ☼ Promotion
- ☼ Dismissals
- ☼ Conditions of employment

The act also **outlines** and **outlaws** the following in the workplace:
- ✿ Harassment
- ✿ Sexual harassment
- ✿ Bullying

Companies must value and promote **equality** and **diversity**. All employees are entitled to equal pay for equal work. The **Equality Authority,** which replaced the Employment Equality Agency, was established under this Act. The act also appointed a **Director of Equality Investigations** to investigate complaints of inequality under the Act.

> **Harassment** is any act or conduct which is offensive, humiliating or intimidating.

Employers are encouraged to put measures in place to promote equality of opportunities. Gender stereotyping involves the assumption that certain jobs are men's jobs and certain jobs are women's.

Young People and Work

Young people have rights and should not be exploited. Both young people and employers should be aware of the Protection of Young Persons (Employment) Act 1996.

The Protection of Young Persons (Employment) Act 1996

> This Act protects young workers' health and ensures that work does not put a young person's education at risk.

DUTIES OF EMPLOYERS

Employers must:
- ✿ See a copy of a **Birth Certificate** before employing someone under 16 and must get the written permission of their parent or guardian.
- ✿ Keep a register containing the following particulars of each person under 18 employed:
  - ▪ Full name
  - ▪ Date of birth
  - ▪ Time work begins each day
  - ▪ Time work ends each day
  - ▪ Rates of wages or salary
  - ▪ Total amount of wages or salary

Age Limit for a Regular Job

For a regular job the minimum age is **16**. For light work employers can hire 14- and 15-year-olds, under the following circumstances:
- ✿ If the work is part-time work (legal at 15 years only)
- ✿ If the work is part of work experience or part of an educational programme
- ✿ During the school holidays, provided there is a minimum three-week break from work in the summer.

Any child under 16 may be employed in film, theatre, sports or advertising under licence.

Maximum Hours of Work Per Week

Under 18's may not be employed for more than **40** hours a week or **8** hours a day, except in a genuine emergency.

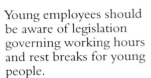

Young employees should be aware of legislation governing working hours and rest breaks for young people.

THE MAXIMUM WEEKLY WORKING HOURS		
	14 years	**15 years**
Term-time	0	8 hours
Holiday work	35 hours	35 hours
Work experience	40 hours	40 hours
NIGHT AND EARLY MORNING WORK		
	Under 16's	**16 and 17**
Night work with school next morning	Up to 8 p.m.	Up to 10 p.m.
No school next morning	Up to 8 p.m.	Up to 10 p.m. and <u>not</u> before 7 a.m.
Early morning	After 8 a.m.	After 6 a.m.
TIME OFF AND REST BREAKS		
	Under 16's	**16 and 17**
30 minutes break after working	4 hours	4.5 hours
Every 24 hours	14 hours off	12 hours off
Every 7 days	2 days off	2 days off

Rights Commissioner

COMPLAINTS

Labour Inspectorate
Department of Enterprise, Trade and Employment

EXCEPTIONS	PENALTIES
○ Work at sea ○ Defence Forces ○ Close relatives/farming	○ A person guilty of an offence under the Act can be fined up to €1,904.61 and an extra €317.43 a day for a continuing offence.

INDUSTRIAL RELATIONS

These are the relationships between employers and employees. It is important to develop and maintain good industrial relations in the workplace. Many organisations promote good industrial relations, e.g. trade unions.

Trade Unions

Examples include:

- **SIPTU** (**S**ervices, **I**ndustrial, **P**rofessional and **T**echnical **U**nion)
- **Impact**
- **TUI** (**T**eachers' **U**nion of **I**reland)
- **ASTI** (**A**ssociation of **S**econdary **T**eachers **I**reland)

Every employee has a legal right, which entitles them to join a trade union.

Functions of a Trade Union

1. They represent the interests of workers in the workplace, e.g. they negotiate for improved wages.
2. They negotiate for improved working conditions, for example:
   - Holidays
   - Hours of work
   - Proper facilities in the workplace, e.g. safe clothing and safety equipment.
3. They negotiate on behalf of members when there are disputes with employers. The trade union will represent employees in these negotiations.
4. National Agreements ensure that all wages are increased by a fixed percentage. Trade unions enter into agreements with the social partners, i.e. the government and employers, on the formation of National Wage Agreements.
5. They provide grants for education.
6. They support and promote equality in the workplace by ensuring that:
   - All employees are treated equally.
   - Employers obey all the equality legislation.
7. They give workers greater strength by uniting them and acting together as one.

Shop Steward

- The Shop Steward is elected by workers to act as their union representative in the workplace.
- He/she recruits new members to the union.
- The Shop Steward keeps members informed of any union developments.
- He/she represents workers in discussions with management.
- The Shop Steward acts as a link between union head office and the workplace.

IBEC – Irish Business and Employers Confederation

This is an organisation which represents employers and businesses.

Conflict

A conflict is a disagreement, a struggle or perhaps a fight.

Why do people disagree?
- They see things differently.
- They want different things.
- Certain personalities clash.

Identify a conflict.

_____
_____
_____
_____
_____
_____
_____
_____

How was this conflict handled?

_____
_____
_____
_____
_____
_____
_____
_____

My suggestions for a successful solution (conflict resolution) are…

_____
_____
_____
_____
_____
_____
_____
_____

Remember, if an issue arises and causes conflict, it must be resolved, otherwise a dispute may result. Conflict may be solved by non-legislative or legislative methods.

ROLE-PLAY

Role-play a situation that could give rise to a **dispute** in the workplace. Prior to attempting the role-play you need to be aware of situations that give rise to a dispute. Think of 3 different situations that could lead to a dispute in the workplace. In each column below list words that relate to that situation.

Situation 1	Situation 2	Situation 3
_____	_____	_____
_____	_____	_____
_____	_____	_____
_____	_____	_____

Role-play is improvising without a script.

Rules for Role-play

* ★ Set objectives.
* ★ Everyone must have a role.
* ★ Do not use bad language.
* ★ Do not permit bullying.
* ★ Do not permit inappropriate personal disclosures.

Role-plays work well for practising interviews and practising conflict resolution.

After the role-play, allow time for **debriefing/evaluating.**
The real value of role-play is in the debriefing. You must document what you learned. It's an excellent way to develop skills, i.e. communication skills, observation skills and interpersonal skills.

DEBRIEFING

After a role-play, you should document the following:

* ★ What happened?
* ★ Link with previous learning.
* ★ What knowledge have I gained?
* ★ What skills did I use/learn?
* ★ What Leaving Certificate subjects were useful?
* ★ List conclusions.

SLO: *You are encouraged to role-play a situation that could give rise to a dispute in the workplace.*

List other **S**pecific **L**earning **O**utcomes, which may be achieved through role-play.

_____

_____

_____

Ideas!
✿ Interviews
✿ Telephone skills

PORTFOLIO ITEM: 'MY OWN PLACE' REPORT

The 'My Own Place' Report is an optional item in the portfolio. It is based on the findings of a local investigation. The report may be based on a single investigation or on a number of events, which have taken place at intervals over the two years of the LCVP.

In investigating 'My Own Place' you should be guided by the **S**pecific **L**earning **O**utcomes in the syllabus. The principal learning outcomes related to 'My Own Place' are the main sources of employment, social services, job creation agencies, transport, financial institutions, industrial relations, economic activities, potential for tourism, and the range of business enterprises, community enterprises and voluntary organisations. 'My Own Place' is broadly defined to provide you with many possibilities depending on your area.

Portfolio Tip:
You may opt to do a Summary Report or a 'My Own Place' Report.

Examples may include:
- ★ Your local town or village
- ★ Your local parish or town land
- ★ The area around your school or your route to school
- ★ Selected locations in a large urban area, e.g., shopping centre, industrial estates

Things to keep in mind

- ★ Optional: As part of your portfolio you must submit a total of **six** items. The report on 'My Own Place' is part of the **optional** items, unless you decide to submit your 'My Own Place' Report as a Summary Report (core item).
- ★ Your report must be presented as a word-processed document (1,000–1,500 words long).
- ★ The report must be your own unique record of the investigation.
- ★ Use simple language, short sentences and short paragraphs.
- ★ Arrange information under clear headings and sub-headings.
- ★ Number pages.
- ★ Use a regular font, such as Times New Roman, size 12pt.
- ★ Keep to a small number of font sizes, e.g. two.

Core
Submit all 4
Optional
Submit 2 out of 4
A total of **6 portfolio items** must be submitted.

Assessment Criteria – Syllabus

The report on 'My Own Place' will assess your ability to:
- ★ Generate a document with a clear and consistent layout.
- ★ Identify the local area under investigation.
- ★ Identify and analyse an important issue relevant to the local area.
- ★ Define the aims/objectives and scope of the investigation.
- ★ Outline the methods used to collect information about the local area.
- ★ Describe an out-of-school group activity undertaken as part of the investigation.
- ★ Analyse the information gathered and select relevant material.
- ★ Use maps, charts, tables, diagrams and pictures, as appropriate to support and illustrate your main findings.
- ★ Link the activity to learning in relevant Leaving Certificate subjects.
- ★ Describe and evaluate your personal contribution to the investigation.
- ★ Draw conclusions and make recommendations appropriate to the investigation.

'My Own Place' Report: Guidelines for Structure

1. **Title Page**
   - A clear **title**, stating that this is a 'My Own Place' Report and identifying the area being investigated, should be included.
   - A **sub-title** may be included to demonstrate greater detail.
   - **Author's name**, i.e your name
   - **For the Attention of,** i.e. mark it for the attention of your teacher
   - **Date**: date of completion, e.g. *20 January 2006*

2. **Table of Contents**
   - List main sections.
   - Give page numbers; these must be accurate.

3. **Introduction**
   - Give a brief **description** of the local area.
   - Outline the **scope** of the investigation, i.e. the aspects being investigated.
   - You could include a **sketch map**, showing the geographical location.

4. **Aims/Objectives**
   - State what you hope to achieve through the activity.
   - Bullet points or numbered lists are recommended.
   - State both group and personal aims.

5. **Body of Report**
   - **Findings**: Describe and analyse key aspects. Arrange findings in a logical sequence under clear headings and subheadings. You may include illustrations or tables.
   - **Research Methods**: Include at least **three** methods.
   - **Out-of-school Activity**: Give date, describe what took place and how the information gained was subsequently used.
   - **Analysis of a Local Issue**: The analysis of a local issue can be dealt with either right through the report (if it was one of your aims) or in the main body of the report (if it was an issue that arose during the investigation).
   - **Link the Learning**: Refer to at least **two** Leaving Certificate subjects, e.g. your **V**ocational **S**ubject **G**roupings. Describe how they were useful.
   - **Personal Contribution**: You can document your personal contribution in one of three ways:
     (a) You can include a paragraph called 'My Personal Contribution'.
     (b) You can highlight your personal contribution in *italics* right through the report.
     (c) You can document it in your evaluation at the end.

6. **Conclusions**
   List your conclusions, and make sure that they relate back to **Aims.**

7. **Recommendations**
   These are suggestions for future actions based on your conclusions.

8. **Evaluation**
   (a) Investigation: Did the group achieve its aims?
   (b) Group activity: How did the group perform?
   (c) Personal performance, if not dealt with separately: How did you perform?

9. **Appendices**: Include a maximum of two items at the end of the report.

'My Own Place' Report: Possible Template for Rough Work

'MY OWN PLACE' REPORT
Title:
Subtitle:
Author's name:
For the Attention of:
Date:
Table of Contents
Introduction
Aims/Objectives
Research Methods

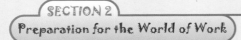

Portfolio Tip: Use the template to record **main points**. Revisit them and elaborate on them at a later stage. Put the template in your LCVP folder.

'My Own Place' Report: Possible Template for Rough Work

Main Findings

Graph/Chart

Local Issue

Link the Learning

My Personal Contribution

Conclusions

Recommendations

Evaluation
    (a) Investigation   (b) Group Performance

Appendices
    (a)   (b)

An Outline of A 'My Own Place' Report Mind Map

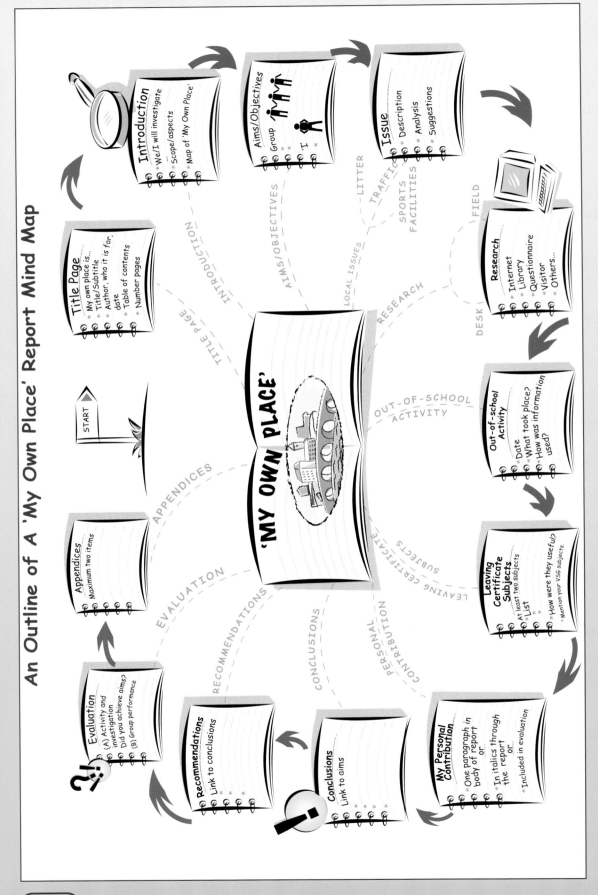

LEARNING BOARD

Briefly summarise the main points using key words from the unit.	Something I **learned**…
_____ _____ _____ _____ _____ _____ _____ _____ _____ _____ _____ _____	_____ _____ _____
	Something I found **difficult**…
	_____ _____ _____
	Write a short **Case Study** relating to unemployment schemes.
	_____ _____ _____

DEVISE AN EXAM QUESTION

Start with a quotation, perhaps a **S**pecific **L**earning **O**utcome or a sentence from this unit.

_____

(a)

(b)

(c)

Write a **6-sentence presentation** on the rights and responsibilities of an employee.

_____
_____
_____
_____
_____
_____

LEARNING BOARD

Can I use this for my **portfolio**?   **Yes** ☐   **No** ☐
The portfolio is worth 60%.

If yes, tick the appropriate box below.

CORE – submit all 4
- ★ Curriculum Vitae ☐
- ★ Career Investigation ☐
- ★ Summary Report ☐
- ★ Enterprise/Action Plan ☐

OPTIONAL – submit 2 out of 4
- ★ Diary of Work Experience ☐
- ★ Enterprise Report ☐
- ★ Recorded Interview/Presentation ☐
- ★ Report on 'My Own Place' ☐

A total of 6 portfolio items must be submitted.

Now that you've worked through this unit, what are the next steps?
_____
_____

What new **skills** have I acquired?	Did I participate in any **teamwork** activities? If yes, specify.	Useful **Websites** www.lcvp.ie www.has.ie www.equality.ie www.welfare.ie Others…

Tasks
- ★ Draft a contract of employment for a job of your choice.
- ★ Choose a local training scheme and write a brief account of this scheme.
- ★ What financial benefits are available to unemployed people?
- ★ Describe the various laws you studied in this unit.

CROSS-CURRICULAR

Cross-curricular learning refers to activities or themes which are relevant to many subjects across the curriculum, e.g. health and safety is important in Chemistry, Construction Studies, Engineering, Home Economics and Business.

- ★ What Leaving Certificate subjects were useful? _____
  _____

- ★ How were they useful? _____
  _____

- ★ Were my **V**ocational **S**ubject **G**roupings useful? _____
  _____

MAKING IT HAPPEN...
PREPARING FOR ASSESSMENT

Assessment ideas based on Preparation for the World of Work
1 – Introduction to Working Life

Portfolio of coursework - 60%

Core

* **Enterprise/Action Plan**
  - Plan a 'My Own Place' investigation.
  - Plan a visit to a training scheme.
  - Plan a visitor to the classroom.
* **Summary Report**
  - 'My Own Place', provided you don't submit a 'My Own Place' Report
  - Visit Out, e.g. to a training scheme
  - Visit In, e.g. from a representative of a training scheme

Options

* **'My Own Place' Report**
* **Recorded Interview/Presentation**
  (a) General interview, 1–2 questions on 'My Own Place'
  (b) Presentation on 'My Own Place'

This unit provides numerous opportunities for plans and reports.

Tip: Use your portfolio as a revision tool for the written paper.

Written Paper - 40%

*Revise the **layout** and **content of your portfolio items**.*

* **SLO's** 1.8-1.14 provide many opportunities to be assessed in the written exam.
  - Differences between school and work
  - Self-employment and voluntary work
  - Legislation – equality, young persons and Safety, Health and Welfare
  - Disputes and diversity in the workplace
  - Assistance for the unemployed
  - Training schemes in the locality
* Revise other aspects of 'My Own Place', for example, sources of employment, social services, job creation, transport, financial institutions, industrial relations, economic activities and potential for tourism.
* Prepare questions that demonstrate that you have participated in an activity. Don't forget to use the **PEP** approach to structure your answer: **P**re-experience, **E**xperience, **P**ost-experience. Part of the learning cycle of the LCVP is planning, participating and evaluating.
* Cross-curricular learning – what Leaving Certificate subjects were useful and how? Refer, in particular, to your **V**ocational **S**ubject **G**roupings.
* Analyse your individual contribution and personal performance.
* Evaluation involves looking at and judging the quality of an activity and asking yourself if you achieved your goals. Consider the following:
  - How and why do we evaluate?
  - Evaluate your 'My Own Place' investigation.
  - Evaluate team performance.

SAMPLE EXAM QUESTIONS

These questions are mostly based on this unit only. In the written paper there may be questions which assess a few units together.

Q.1 Working life is explored in the LCVP.
(a)   Describe the functions of a trade union.
(b)   State personal qualities which a local employer would look for in an employee.
(c)   Draft a contract of employment to be given to a new employee.
(d)   Comment on the differences between school and work.

Q.2 Everyone is engaged in either paid or unpaid work.
(a)   Describe the benefits to be gained from participation in work and list the different types of work you are involved in.
(b)   Discuss recent changes in employment.
(c)   Identify reasons for conflict in the workplace and recommend ways of successfully resolving such conflicts.
(d)   Outline two different schemes in operation to help the unemployed return to work.

Q.3 Working life and local employment opportunities are investigated in the LCVP.
(a)   Identify the main social services and job creation agencies in the local area you studied during the LCVP.
(b)   Describe how you planned for your local area investigation.
(c)   Outline your understanding of diversity in the workplace.
(d)   List some useful resources for a 'My Own Place' investigation.

Q.4 Many voluntary organisations rely on people to work for nothing.
(a)   Compare paid employment with voluntary work.
(b)   Describe a voluntary organisation in your locality.
(c)   Draft a letter to a representative of a local training scheme, inviting them to the LCVP class. Outline in your letter your reasons for wanting to organise a Visit In.
(d)   List the ways you can evaluate a Visit Out and explain the advantages of evaluation.

Q.5 When leaving school to start your working life, you will face a lot of challenges.
(a)   Describe any laws which you have studied in the Link Modules which are relevant to you as an employee.
(b)   List two Leaving Certificate subjects (excluding the Link Modules), which are useful in the world of work. Outline how they are useful.
(c)   Indicate the advantages of self-employment.
(d)   Identify opportunities for work in your local area.

LINK MODULE 1 – PREPARATION FOR THE WORLD OF WORK

UNIT 2 – JOB-SEEKING SKILLS

The aim of this unit is to equip you with the skills and confidence necessary to gain employment and to develop your organisational and communicative skills. The involvement of adults from business and the local community is recommended in order to help you gain practice in presenting yourself to prospective employers.

SPECIFIC LEARNING OUTCOMES – SLOs

(as listed in the syllabus)

When you have finished working through this unit, you should be able to:

2.1	recognise the different ways in which job vacancies are advertised
2.2	apply for a job by letter, telephone and e-mail
2.3	complete an application form
2.4	compile and create a curriculum vitae in word-processed format
2.5	explain how to prepare for a job interview
2.6	engage in a simulated job interview

Work is an integral part of our lives and everyone is seeking the ideal type of **work**. Work can be paid or unpaid but there are many benefits:

- Wages are received for paid work.
- Self-esteem rises and a sense of achievement is enjoyed when you do something worthwhile.
- There is always the possibility of promotion.
- Employees have a chance to improve skills.
- Opportunities to travel can arise.

There are certain **qualities** that help make a person more employable:

1. **Energy, drive and hard work**: when employees show interest and overcome difficulties.
2. **Reliability**: when employees can be trusted and depended on.
3. **Enthusiasm and commitment**: when employees show interest, eagerness, dedication and responsibility.
4. **Adaptability**: when employees are flexible and can accept change.
5. **Good education**: when employees have qualifications and experience.

What qualities do I have?

RECRUITMENT

Recruiting is more then just placing an advertisement and interviewing. It starts with deciding how to recruit (you could use an agency or recruit via newspapers/websites etc.), making job descriptions and application forms, assessing CVs, short-listing candidates, interviewing, selecting and checking references.

Selecting and retaining the right staff is critical to your business's success.

Decide on a job description before recruiting. The job description defines the purpose, role and responsibilities of the position. It also describes the education, qualifications, qualities, experience and skills that an individual needs in order to get the job.

What methods can an **employer** use to recruit?

- Employers can advertise in newspapers or on television, radio, Aertel, on the Internet or on notice boards.
- They can use a recruitment agency.
- They can hire someone who has done work experience with them.
- They can use contacts.
- They can organise recruitment fairs/recruitment days.
- They can approach job training agencies, e.g. FÁS.
- They can hope that word will spread that they are looking for somebody (word of mouth).
- They can network to find the right person.

Reasons for Vacancies

- The business could be expanding.
- Employees could be retiring.
- Employees could be leaving.
- The company may need to replace employees who are absent due to sick/maternity leave or career breaks.
- Seasonal work may have arisen.

Front Desk Receptionist Required
An experienced front desk receptionist is required for the Ballycastle Bay Hotel, Co. Mayo.
We are looking for ambitious, career-minded individuals.

An employee may seek a job by **Networking**, which involves finding out about vacancies through friends, family and professional contacts.

Difficulties for Employers when Recruiting

Sometimes it can prove difficult to fill a position. This can occur for a variety of reasons:

1. The work itself may be dull or boring.
2. There may be a skills shortage in that field.
3. General economic conditions may make it difficult to recruit, e.g. low unemployment means people become fussier about the kind of work they want to do.
4. The location of the business may make it awkward for employees to get to work.
5. Wages and working conditions may not be attractive.

Ways to Overcome Recruitment Problems

1. Recruit from abroad.
2. Offer part-time work, job-sharing and flexitime.
3. Provide training opportunities and grants for further education.
4. Provide accommodation.
5. Link up with local schools/colleges.

Recruitment Agencies

The success of any business is dependent on the people it employs. Using a recruitment agency can help you find the ideal employees.

Benefits of using Recruitment Agencies

1. Recruitment agencies offer a full range of services related to recruitment, such as advertising, profiling, interviewing, short-listing, selection, checking references and, if required, drawing up contracts of employment. This can save time and money.
2. Good recruitment agencies attract high calibre applicants.
3. Agencies have specialised staff that will recruit more objectively.

> Certain jobs are declining:
> • Farmers
> • Typists
> • Sewing machine operators
> • Switchboard operators

APPLYING FOR A JOB

Usually a candidate will apply for a job using one or more of the following:

- ☼ Letter
- ☼ Telephone
- ☼ E-mail
- ☼ Application form
- ☼ Curriculum Vitae

> Advertising helps to target the best people for the job.

Advertisement

Campbell Communications is looking for young dynamic salespeople to join its sales team. Campbell Communications is one of the most prestigious mobile distributors.

The successful candidates must have:
- Excellent IT skills
- Excellent communications and interpersonal skills
- Good team skills

For an application form and further information,
contact **Campbell Communications** at:
1399, The Mall, Athlone.
Telephone 0906 3425157 e-mail: cc@eircom.net

Using adverts you've sourced from local newspapers or using the Campbell Communications advert above, fill in the following worksheet:

★ **What** job is being advertised?	★ **When** was it advertised?
★ **Who** is advertising?	★ **Where** was it advertised?

JOB SPECIFICATIONS	MY PROFILE
Skills/Qualities	Skills/Qualities
Experience	Experience
Qualifications	Qualifications

Am I suitable for the job?   Yes ☐   No ☐

If no, what do I need to do to meet the specifications?

Applying for a Job by Telephone

Often an advertisement may ask you to phone for an application form or to arrange an appointment. This phone call can sometimes turn into a short telephone interview. It is important, therefore, to make sure you're prepared **before you phone**.

Pre-telephoning

- Have the advertisement and your CV in front of you.
- Ideally, you should phone from a landline in a quiet room, rather than from a public phone or mobile phone.
- Have a pen and paper ready to record any important information.
- Make sure you know the times and dates that you are available for interview.

While Telephoning

- Speak clearly, confidently and slowly, giving your name and your reason for calling.
- Ask to speak to the person whose contact details were given in the advertisement.
- Record relevant information.
- Listen attentively to questions and ask to have them repeated if you don't understand them.
- If left waiting, remain calm.
- Ask for directions if necessary.
- Keep the conversation brief.
- Thank the receiver for his/her time.

Sometimes you may reach an answering machine, so it is important to have prepared in advance a short, clear message with your name and contact details.

Post-telephoning

- Re-read your notes and make sure you understand what was said.
- Record the date and the name of the person you spoke to.
- Record the time and date of the interview in your diary.

ACTIVITY

In pairs, role-play 'applying for a job by telephone' without a script. Allow a maximum of ten minutes. Give feedback on the role-play.

Document learning using your **LCVP folder** and remember the PEP learning approach: Pre-experience, Experience and Post-experience.

Letter of Application

The purpose of a letter of application is to introduce yourself to a prospective employer and hopefully obtain an interview. Since the letter of application is the first point of contact between you and the company, it is essential that it is of the highest possible standard. The person recruiting will read the letter before they look at your CV and application form and you want to make sure that you make a good impression.

The letter should highlight the most important points in your CV, in particular, your strengths and suitability for the job. It should also explain why you are applying for this position.

Tips for Letter Writing

- Letters should be typed (unless the advert specifically asks for handwritten letters) and no longer than one page.
- Use high quality, clean, white A4-size paper.
- Use black ink.
- Do not use Tipp-Ex: if you make a mistake, start again.
- Do not send a photocopy.
- Keep words, sentences and paragraphs short.
- Use Times New Roman and always do a spell-check.

Tip: Practise letter writing, e.g. write a letter to thank a visitor, to arrange a visit out, or to arrange a work placement.

Layout of a Letter

1. **Address of writer**: Your address and telephone number should be in the top right-hand corner of the page. Check punctuation and give your area code. Leave a gap.
2. **Date**: Include date, e.g. 12 September 2005.
3. **Name and Address of Recipient**: This appears on the left-hand side of the page.
4. **Subject Line**: Define the reason you are writing the letter.
5. **Salutation**: Address the person you're writing to, e.g. *Dear Mrs Togher.* This is followed by a comma (,).
6. The **Body** of the letter.
    - (a) **Beginning**: Introduce yourself and refer to the name and date of the advertisement.
    - (b) **Middle**: State your skills, qualities and experience and explain your interest in the job.
    - (c) **End**: The end of the letter should be positive and confident. Mention the dates and times that you're available for interview and say that you're looking forward to hearing from him/her.
7. **Complementary Close**: In other words, how you close depends on how you open the letter. If you open with *Dear Sir/Madam*, you close with *Yours faithfully*. If you know the name of the person and open with it (e.g. *Dear Mrs Togher*), you close with *Yours sincerely.*
8. Insert a space, followed by your **Signature**.
9. Type your **Name and Title** (Mr, Mrs, Ms).
10. **Enc**: Mention here anything you're sending with the letter, e.g. a reference.

> In the written paper, if asked to write a letter, you must keep to a **formal layout** and also apply any **relevant text** given in the exam question.

Sample Layout

(1) Address of Writer

(2) Date

Day Month Year

(3) Name, Position &
Address of Recipient

(4) Subject Line: 'Re: advertised position'

(5) Dear Mrs O'Connell,

(6a) Beginning: 'With reference to your advertisement ...'

(6b) Middle: Skills ... (Refer to the text in question.)

(6c) End: 'I look forward to hearing from you.'

(7) Yours sincerely,

(8) Signature

(9) Name Typed

(10) Enc.

Sample Letter

70 Ocean View,
Church Road,
Belmullet,
Co. Mayo.
Tel: 097-228202

25 March 2006

Mr J. Maher,
The Personnel Manager,
Kent Communications,
23 Halpin Road,
Balydoyle,
Dublin 13.

Re: Application for Store Manager

Dear Mr Maher,

I wish to apply for the position of Store Manager as advertised in the Irish Independent on Thursday, 22 March 2006.

I am a 21-year-old business student, who is currently participating in a management course with Cert. I achieved first-class honours in my Business degree with Sligo IT. I work on a part-time basis with Castle Computer stores. I am hard-working and creative with excellent interpersonal skills.

I would appreciate the opportunity to meet and discuss the matter further with you. I am available for interview at any time that's convenient to you.

I look forward to hearing from you.

Yours sincerely,

Steven Gallagher

Steven Gallagher

Enc: Curriculum Vitae

Application Forms

Most application forms are simple documents that basically just ask for the information contained in your CV: personal details, qualifications, skills etc. Some forms are, however, more detailed and require much more thought. You may be asked to explain why you're suitable for the job, for example; this can help to prepare you for the interview.

They are designed to obtain standard information about every applicant and they don't allow for flexibility. Sometimes they are poorly designed and don't allow enough space for your answer.

Note: Keep a copy of your application form so that you can look at it before your interview.

Guidelines for Successful Form Filling

- Read the form carefully and thoroughly.
- Have your CV beside you so that you can copy from it.
- Photocopy the form and practise filling it in.
- Begin with the easiest questions.
- Draft the answers to complex questions on a rough piece of paper.
- Fill in ALL the boxes truthfully. Do not fill in sections marked 'For Office Use Only'.
- If a question doesn't apply to you, write in 'N/A' for 'not applicable'.
- Double-check that there aren't any spelling/grammatical errors.
- Start filling in the real application form.
- Use a black pen and BLOCK CAPITAL LETTERING.
- Do not use Tipp-Ex or similar correction products.
- Make sure your hands are clean before handling the form, and keep it in pristine condition.
- Keep a photocopy of the completed form so that you can look over it if you're called for an interview.
- Other points _____

You may be asked questions about form filling in the revised Link Modules exam.

ACTIVITY

Practise the above guidelines with:

- ★ Job application form
- ★ Passport application form
- ★ Provisional licence form
- ★ Driving theory test form
- ★ Driving test form

Useful Words

WORDS ON APPLICATION FORMS

Title:	Miss, Ms, Mrs, Mr, Dr
Christian Name:	First name, e.g. Mike, Conor, Lil, Shelagh, Marion or Ciara
Surname:	Your family name, e.g. Carew, Walsh, Daly, Hand
Temporary Address:	Where you live at the moment
Home/Permanent Address:	For example, your parents' address
Nationality:	Refers to the country you were born in, e.g. Ireland/Irish
Marital Status:	This refers to your status, e.g. single, married, widowed.
Next of Kin:	Your closest relative, e.g. wife, husband, mother etc.
Referee:	Name, address and phone number of a person who knows you well and will recommend you for the job. You would usually ask your previous employer to be your referee.

Remember you must get permission from referees beforehand and keep them informed about what you are applying for.

Signed:	This is where you must put your signature in your own handwriting, e.g. Gearoíd Hourihan.

Most application forms have a box at the end for you to include additional information. This is your opportunity to include anything you have not had a chance to say in the main body of the form.

The computer input type form is becoming more popular, e.g. you can now e-mail your CAO application to their office. The same guidelines apply to using e-mail, i.e. politeness, contact address etc.

Sample Job Application Form

Using your guidelines for success in form filling, complete the following job application form. Remember you may also have to complete an application form in the written paper.

Please complete all sections in your own handwriting. Use BLOCK CAPITALS.			
Position applied for:			
Surname:		First names:	
Present Address:			
Home Address (If different to above):			
Home Telephone No:		Work Telephone No:	
E-mail Address:			
Date of Birth:		Nationality:	
Education			
School/Colleges	Years	Examinations Taken	Results
Reasons for Applying for the Position:			

Sample Job Application Form

Work Experience (Starting with your most recent employment).			
Dates	Employer	Position	Reason for Leaving

Interests/Hobbies:

Any Additional Information:

Referee:	Referee:

I declare that the information contained in this document is correct.

Signature: _____ Date: _____

Curriculum Vitae

The initials CV stand for the Latin **Curriculum Vitae**, meaning 'course of life'. A CV is a summary of your education, skills and experience. The purpose of a CV is to help you get an interview for a job. Although there is no one right layout or template, a CV will typically contain the applicant's personal details, qualifications, qualities and skills, work experience, achievements and interests.

In your portfolio, you should not reproduce a CV for a particular job. You should compose a **general, all-purpose CV** that concentrates on presenting relevant information in a concise and ordered way. For the portfolio, you are encouraged to show evidence of new skills and experience gained during the programme.

Tip: continually update your personal statement as you participate in activities.

Skills and Qualities

You may find it difficult to identify and document your skills and qualities. The following ideas might help you.

- Do a **skills audit** (see p. 91) to measure your practical, technical and interpersonal skills.
- Do a **multiple intelligences test** (see p. 93).
- As you **participate in activities** during the course of the LCVP, keep note of the skills you developed and the qualities you demonstrated.

When presenting your skills and qualities in your CV, you may decide to write a personal statement **or** you may prefer to present them as bullet points.

You can present your skills and qualities as a personal statement **or** as bulleted points.

Statement

Below are some examples of personal statements of skills and qualities.

'An enthusiastic, self-motivated student, who always strives to achieve a very high standard.'
'A good team member with excellent communication skills.'
'A determined, honest and trustworthy school leaver with the ability to motivate others.'

A **personal profile/statement** says what is special about you.

My Personal Statement

You may decide to continually **update** your personal statement as you engage in LCVP activities. This will help you write your statement of skills and qualities.

Bullet Points

Personal Skills and Qualities

- Good communication skills
- Flexible and willing to learn
- Good organisational skills
- Very creative

Do not copy the above. Ensure your skills and qualities are related to the content of your CV.

PORTFOLIO ITEM: CURRICULUM VITAE (CV)

Things to keep in mind

* Compulsory: As part of your portfolio, you must submit a total of **six** items. Your CV is part of the **mandatory** core.
* Your CV must be word-processed.
* Categorise information under appropriate headings.
* The information in your CV must be accurate, factual and concise.
* Your CV should not exceed two A4 pages.
* Use a regular font such as Times New Roman, size 12pt.

> **Core**
> Submit all 4
> **Optional**
> Submit 2 out of 4
> A total of **6 portfolio items** must be submitted.

Assessment Criteria – Syllabus

The **Curriculum Vitae** will assess your ability to:
* Generate a word-processed document with a clean and consistent layout.
* Choose fonts, format and language appropriate to the task content.
* Select relevant information, present it in categories under appropriate headings, and arrange it in appropriate order.
* Communicate concisely and accurately using correct grammar, spelling and punctuation.
* Highlight personal skills and qualities in an imaginative way.

CV: Guidelines for Structure

1. **Personal Details**

   These may include name, address, telephone number and date of birth. A student is not required to give details such as nationality, gender or religion on the CV and may prefer not to show date of birth. The CV must be **signed** and **dated**.

2. **Education/Qualifications**

   This will include **names of schools** attended, **years** attended and **dates** of examinations and **subjects** taken, including levels and grades. In the majority of cases, the examinations will comprise the Junior Certificate (results) and the Leaving Certificate (to be taken). Don't forget to include the **Link Modules**.

3. **Work Experience**

   Start with the **most recent** job/work placement you have done, giving the dates of employment, the name of the employer and their address. Give a brief summary of **responsibilities**.

4. **Achievements**

   Give information about specific achievements. These might be school related, personal or sporting achievements.

5. **Interests and Hobbies**

   Select examples which demonstrate skills or abilities to a prospective employer.

6. **Additional Information**

   Any further information which might support an application, such as membership of an organisation or the ability to speak another language, should be included here.

7. **Referees**

   You should give the names, job titles, addresses and telephone numbers of **two referees**.

8. **Your Signature and the Date**

   Mary Mc Laughlin, 10 April 2006

9. **Skills and Qualities**

   The assessment criteria for the Link Modules require you to **highlight personal skills and qualities in an imaginative way**. Write a short statement like the example below.

'A hard-working, self-motivated school leaver, with good communication and organisation skills and a high level of interpersonal skills'

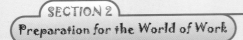

Curriculum Vitae: Possible Template for Rough Work

Curriculum Vitae

Insert your personal statement in this box.

Personal Details

Name:

Address:

Telephone No:

E-mail Address:

Education

Primary School:

Post Primary:

Examinations

Junior Certificate (20_ _)

Subject	Level	Grade

Tip: For subject level you may use H for Higher level and O for Ordinary level.

Leaving Certificate (20_ _)

Subject	Level	Grade

*Tip: Don't forget that **Link Modules** is a Leaving Certificate Subject.*

Curriculum Vitae:
Possible Template for Rough Work

Work Experience

Date:
Employer:

Duties:

Date:
Employer:

Duties:

Tip: Use this template to record your details, then type your CV. Be sure to keep a back-up copy as you may wish to make changes. The word-processed CV should be **error free – perfect!**

Interests and Hobbies

Achievements

Referee	**Referee**

Tip: Don't forget to include two referees and state their positions.

Signed: _____   Date: _____

SAMPLE PORTFOLIO ITEM

CURRICULUM VITAE

Curriculum Vitae

'A hard-working, self-motivated school leaver, with good communication and organisational skills and a high level of interpersonal skills'

Michael O'Malley

Personal Details
Name:
Address:

Michael O'Malley
6 Church View,
Claregalway,
Co. Galway.

Telephone: 091 9727660
E-mail: michaelomalley@eircom.net

Education
Primary School 1992–2000: St. John's National School, Galway
Post-primary 2000–2006: Colaiste Eoin, Galway

Examinations

Junior Certificate 2003

Subject	Level	Grade
English	Higher	B
Gaeilge	Ordinary	C
Maths	Ordinary	A
History	Higher	B
Geography	Higher	A
Science	Higher	C
Music	Higher	A
Art	Ordinary	B
nch	Common	C
P.E.		A

Leaving Certificate 2006

Level	Grade
Higher	
Ordinary	
Ordinary	
Higher	
Higher	
Higher	
Higher	
Common	

Work Experience

Part-time Music Teacher
Job Title: 25 September 2005–Present (Saturdays only)
Date: Galway School of Music,
Employer: Georges St,
Galway
Duties:
• Teaching drums in one-to-one and group classes
• Organising schedules for class times
• Preparing grade examinations

Administrative Assistant
Job Title: 1 July–30 August 2005 and 27–30 October 2005
Date: O'Reilly Accountants
Employer: Patrick's Court,
Patrick Street,
Galway City
Duties:
• Collecting and filing customer accounts
• Typing letters
• Inputting and adding figures on the computer
• Photocopying standard acccounting letters
• Making corrections to accounts

Interests and Hobbies
• I have a very strong interest in music. I play the drums/percussion, guitar and piano. I have dedicated much of my time to teaching, learning and performing.
• I play football and hurling for my local G.A.A. club and for my school. I am a member of the local golf club. I also follow the Galway rugby clubs.

Achievements
• I have received the Grade 8 Musical Qualification for Drum Kit and for Percussion from The London College of Music and the Royal Irish Academy.
• Senior Prefect 2005 – 2006
• Head-Boy 2005 – 2006

Referees
Ms Martina Waldron,
Principal,
Colaiste Eoin,
Galway.

Tel: 091 9425678

Mr Eoin Garvey,
Owner and Manager,
Galway School of Music,
Georges Street,
Galway.
Tel: 091 9478954

Date: 21st March 2006

Signed: Michael O'Malley
Michael O'Malley

PREPARING FOR AN INTERVIEW

A good cover letter, application form and CV will get you an interview, but you need to do an **excellent interview** to get the job. Employers are trying to find the most suitable person. You must persuade them that you are the best person for the job. **Remember,** your CV and application form show your education, work experience, training accomplishments, skills and qualities. References show your personal qualities and characteristics. Interviews are, however, the deciding factor. You come face to face with your potential employer and you have to prove yourself.

There are many types of interviews. They vary tremendously, but the success of an interview depends on planning.

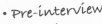

- Pre-interview
- Interview
- Post-interview

Pre-interview

- You need to be prepared: research the job and the workplace – use the Internet to do this. Update your CV, making sure to add any new qualifications.
- Practise possible questions and responses. Role-play an interview. Always stress the positive in your answers to questions.
- Organise what to wear and dress neatly and appropriately. Aim for a well-groomed and clean appearance.
- Plan to get to the interview on time. Consider doing a 'dummy run' the day before to check how long it will take you. Allow for delays.
- Know your strengths and weaknesses. Do a **SWOT analysis**.

During the Interview

- Start with a firm handshake and a smile.
- Establish and maintain eye contact during the interview.
- Communicate positively, clearly and with confidence.
- Sit with both feet on the floor and don't slouch.
- Listen attentively and answer truthfully. Ask for questions to be repeated if you don't understand them.
- Expect the unexpected, e.g. awkward or difficult questions.
- Thank the interviewer for taking the time to meet you.

I can be a bit impatient sometimes, but that means that I always meet my deadlines.

Make weaknesses look like strengths.

Post-interview

If you don't get the job, evaluate the interview and consider what improvements could be made for the next interview. Contact the company and find out how you performed. Try to look at it as a learning experience, which will help you at your next interview.

Evaluating an Interview

The following questions may help you to evaluate your interview:
- What was the best part of the interview?
- What could I have improved on?
- Any additional things I would have liked the employer to know?

Revise Evaluation.

ACTIVITY

Take an advertisement for a job from a newspaper. First of all, brainstorm your skills and qualities generally. Then, focus on which of those skills and qualities would be relevant for this job

MY SKILLS	MY QUALITIES	Which of my skills/qualities are relevant for this job?

Which skills are **transferable**, i.e. which skills can be applied to any job?

_____
_____
_____
_____

List possible questions that could be asked at an interview.

_____
_____
_____
_____

What questions would be appropriate for the interviewee to ask?

_____
_____
_____
_____

ROLE-PLAY

Role-play a job interview in pairs without a script.
Document the learning.

LEARNING BOARD

Briefly summarise the main points using key words from the unit.

Something I **learned**…

Something I found **difficult**…

Write a short **Case Study** relating to job-seeking skills.

DEVISE AN EXAM QUESTION

Start with a quotation, perhaps a **S**pecific **L**earning **O**utcome or a sentence from this unit.

(a)

(b)

(c)

Write a **6-sentence presentation** on recruitment.

LEARNING BOARD

Can I use this for my **portfolio**?   **Yes** ☐   **No** ☐
The portfolio is worth 60%.

If yes, tick the appropriate box below.

CORE – submit all 4

* Curriculum Vitae ☐
* Career Investigation ☐
* Summary Report ☐
* Enterprise/Action Plan ☐

OPTIONAL – submit 2 out of 4

* Diary of Work Experience ☐
* Enterprise Report ☐
* Recorded Interview/Presentation ☐
* Report on 'My Own Place' ☐

A total of 6 portfolio items must be submitted.

Now that you've worked through this unit, what are the next steps?

_____

_____

What new **skills** have I acquired?	Did I participate in any **teamwork** activities? If yes, specify.	Useful **Websites** www.irishjobs.ie www.recruitment.com www.failteireland.ie Others…
_____	_____	
_____	_____	

Tasks

* Draft an advertisement for the position of **manager** of a local recruitment agency.
* List questions you may be asked at an interview for a job of your choice.
* What advice would you give to someone preparing for an interview?
* Explain what **referees** are and why they are important.
* Write a letter applying for an LCVP work placement.
* What advice would you give to someone filling out an application form for the first time?

CROSS-CURRICULAR

Cross-curricular learning refers to activities or themes which are relevant to many subjects across the curriculum, e.g. health and safety is important in Chemistry, Construction Studies, Engineering, Home Economics and Business.

* What Leaving Certificate subjects were useful? _____

_____

* How were they useful? _____

_____

* Were my **V**ocational **S**ubject **G**roupings useful? _____

_____

MAKING IT HAPPEN... PREPARING FOR ASSESSMENT

Assessment ideas based on Preparation for the World of Work
Unit 2 – Job-Seeking Skills

Portfolio of coursework – 60%

Core

* **Enterprise/Action Plan**
  - Plan for a job interview.
* **Curriculum Vitae**
* **Summary Report**
  - Job interviews

Options

* **Recorded Interview/Presentation**
  (a) General interview: 1–2 questions on job-seeking skills.
  (b) Presentation on job-seeking skills.

Written Paper – 40%

Tip: Use your portfolio as a revision tool for the written paper.

*Revise the **layout** and **content of your portfolio items**.*
* Revise the following topics as well:
  - How are jobs advertised?
  - Write a letter, making sure you use a formal layout.
  - How to prepare for a job interview.
  - How firms recruit, the benefits of using recruitment agencies, why employers sometimes have difficulties recruiting and how to overcome these difficulties.
  - How to apply for a job by telephone.
  - Tips for letter writing.
  - Guidelines for success in form filling.
  - Discuss transferable skills.
* Prepare for questions that demonstrate that you have participated in an activity e.g. an interview. Don't forget to use the **PEP** approach to structure your answer: **P**re-experience, **E**xperience, **P**ost-experience.
* Cross-curricular learning – what Leaving Certificate subjects were useful and how? Discuss, in particular, your **V**ocational **S**ubject **G**roupings.
* Analyse your individual contribution and personal performance.
* Evaluation involves looking at and judging the quality of an activity and asking yourself if you achieved your goals. Consider the following:
  - How and why do we evaluate?
  - Evaluate an activity.
  - Evaluate group performance/teamwork.

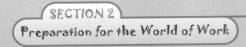

SAMPLE EXAM QUESTIONS

These questions are mostly based on this unit only. In the written paper there may be questions which assess a few units together.

Q.1 Application forms can be simple documents seeking everyday details or they can be lengthy, thought-provoking documents.
(a) Name four different application forms you encountered during the LCVP.
(b) Describe the advice you would give to someone filling out an application form.
(c) Indicate how an employer can recruit employees.
(d) Write a paragraph outlining how you would prepare for an interview.

Q.2 Applying for a job involves many different stages.
(a) Explain two rights and responsibilities of an employee.
(b) Discuss how you can make a good impression at an interview.
(c) List three questions you could be asked at a job interview and write a brief response to each question.
(d) Draft a letter requesting an application form.

Q.3

Heskin Ltd is looking for dynamic young salespeople to join its sales team. Heskin Ltd is one of the best-known health research companies. The successful candidates must have:

>Excellent IT skills
>Excellent communications and interpersonal skills
>Energy and good team skills

For an application form and further information, contact David Heskin at
>Heskin Ltd,
>111 The Mall,
>Western Road,
>Cork.
>e-mail: dheskin/rd@eircom.net
>phone: 021 2345678

(a) Write a letter requesting an application form.
(b) Describe how you can make a good impression at an interview.
(c) Discuss how to prepare for an interview.
(d) Comment on the future of work.

LINK MODULE 1 – PREPARATION FOR THE WORLD OF WORK

UNIT 3 – CAREER INVESTIGATION

This unit introduces the skills of career research and planning. You will be encouraged to investigate careers that suit your interests and abilities and that are relevant to your choice of Leaving Certificate subjects, with particular reference to your selected Vocational Subject Groupings.

SPECIFIC LEARNING OUTCOMES – SLOs

(as listed in the syllabus)

When you have finished working through this unit, you should be able to:

3.1	identify personal aptitudes and interests
3.2	investigate a range of careers appropriate to personal aptitude and interests
3.3	identify and analyse the aptitude and skills required to pursue a specific career
3.4	describe relevant qualifications and training required for entry to the selected career
3.5	identify available opportunities to pursue a selected career locally, nationally, and where possible, at international level
3.6	plan and set up an opportunity to interview and/or work shadow a person in a selected career.
3.7	integrate information from a variety of sources to prepare a final report on a career investigation
3.8	reflect on and evaluate the experience of undertaking a career investigation
3.9	link the activities in this unit to learning in relevant Leaving Certificate subjects

A **Career Investigation** introduces you to the **skills of researching** a career. Ideally, you should look into a career that is related to your interests, your aptitudes (talents and abilities), and to your choice of Leaving Certificate subjects, with particular reference to your **V**ocational **S**ubject **G**roupings. Before you can do that, you need to become aware of what your abilities, interests and talents are. Only then can you evaluate the vocational options open to you. As you will have to change jobs many times throughout your career, you will also need to know how to access information about career opportunities.

> Start by completing a **personal profile**, stating your aptitudes, skills, qualities, experiences, subjects and work preferences.

You may research **many careers,** but for the portfolio assessment you show only **one career** that you have researched for your portfolio entry.

To start with, you will need to do the following:

- Assess your skills, qualities, aptitudes, interests and work preferences.
- Find out how information relating to your career choice can be accessed.
- Research the qualifications and training required for that particular job.
- Draw up a contingency plan.
- Interview and/or work shadow someone in your chosen career.

The Career Investigation is a summary of the information gathered and insights gained while researching your chosen career. The ability to research and plan a career is essential for future employees because you may find that you often have to change employment during your working life. The ability to access information about career opportunities and evaluate your options is a **lifelong skill**. Remember, it's important to engage in a Career Investigation in conjunction with your **Guidance Counsellor** and other counselling activities in the school.

CHOOSING A CAREER

Deciding on your career may be the most important decision that you ever have to make.

> You must match your skills, interests and abilities with the options that are available.

Use fifth year as a time to identify your skills and aptitudes. Talk to your Guidance Counsellor and try to get some work experience or a work shadow in a particular area that you are interested in. Interview a person in your selected career. **Research** is the key to success when it comes to making an informed decision about your future.

Stages of a Career Investigation
- Compile a personal profile.
- Select your preferred job and conduct research, e.g. career path, skills, qualities, training and qualifications necessary.
- Interview and/or work shadow in your chosen career.
- Submit a Career Investigation in accordance with the assessment criteria and guidelines.

> This may be assessed in the written exam.

Skills Audit

You have to become aware of the skills that you have, both as an individual (i.e. when you're working alone) and/or as part of a team (i.e. when you work with others). The skills that you demonstrate often depend on the activity that you're engaged in. Participating in a skills audit highlights your highs and also your lows (i.e. skills that need to be developed).

Skills Audit

Tick the boxes (✓) that apply to you. This may come up in the written exam.

Personal Skills/Qualities
I am...

Honest	
Dependable	
Willing to learn	
Confident and determined	✓
Creative	✓
Self-motivated	
Aware of my strengths	✓
Humorous	
Friendly and sociable	✓
Organised with my time	
Ready to admit mistakes	
Accepting of criticism	✓
Comfortable expressing my opinion	✓

HIGHS

My top 3 personal skills are:

_____

_____

_____

LOWS

What personal skills can I improve on?

self motaveted

_____

Technical/Practical Skills
I am good at...

Writing reports and letters	
Foreign languages	
Computer skills	✓
Researching	✓
Managing money	
Numbers	✓
Generating ideas	✓
Designing	
Speaking on the telephone	
Working with my hands	
Knowledge of materials	
Making things	✓
Cooking	

HIGHS

My top 3 technical skills are:

_____

_____

_____

LOWS

What technical skills can I improve on?

managing money

_____

Interpersonal/Group Skills
I can...

Work well with others	✓
Communicate well and listen to others	
Lead others/Chair meeting	
Allow others to lead	
Deal with conflict	✓
Teach skills to others	
Meet and greet strangers	
Seek the opinion of others	✓
Ensure others are heard	✓
Speak in front of a group	✓
Follow the ideas of others	✓
Encourage others	✓
Get on with authority	✓

HIGHS

My top 3 interpersonal skills are:

_____

_____

_____

LOWS

What interpersonal skills can I work on?

_____

Multiple Intelligences: Identifying Your Strengths and Weaknesses

Dr Howard Gardner, a Harvard psychologist, identified at least eight types of intelligences. He was dissatisfied with the narrow range of ability that IQ tests measured. Gardner studied different cultures, brain-damaged adults and autistic children. He wanted to devise a broader concept of intelligence and come up with at least eight systems of learning. Some people excel in one of the eight intelligences at the expense of others, while others have a more balanced profile. Determining your **strengths** and then using them to boost your **weaknesses** can help you to improve your performance in school, further education, your chosen career and in the world of work.

Gardner's eight types of intelligences are:

Logical/Mathematical

- Good at numbers
- Likes to experiment and solve problems
- Enjoys working with formulae
- Loves the challenge of a complex problem

$$e=mc^2$$

Linguistic/Verbal

- Good at rhythms and meanings of words
- Likes to read, write and listen
- Enjoys writing stories
- Loves to spell words

Musical

- Good at reproducing melodies
- Likes to have music in the background
- Enjoys music and rhythmic patterns
- Loves mimicking sounds

Spatial/Visual

- Good with colours
- Likes to think in images and pictures
- Enjoys day-dreaming
- Loves jigsaws and reading maps

Kinaesthetic/Body

- Good at handling objects
- Likes to touch, feel and tap
- Enjoys role-play and physical exercise
- Loves movement

Interpersonal

- Good at communicating with others
- Likes to work in groups
- Enjoys listening and handling conflicts
- Loves to respond to the needs of others

Intrapersonal

- Good at thinking
- Likes to work alone
- Enjoys reflecting and keeping a journal
- Loves meditation

Naturalist

- Good at noticing patterns in the environment
- Likes to collect items from nature
- Loves distinguishing different things in the natural world

A Fun Quiz to Spot your Strongest Intelligence

Read the statements below and then quickly tick the ones that are **true** for you.
Document your score out of 10.

Linguistic/Verbal Intelligence

- ☑ I enjoy playing with words and doing tongue twisters.
- ☐ I enjoy doing crosswords and anagrams and playing word games like Scrabble.
- ☑ I sometimes use words that other people don't know.
- ☐ I remember the slogans and words from ads more than the pictures/images.
- ☐ I love reading books.
- ☑ I find subjects like English easier than Maths or Accounting.
- ☐ I enjoy talking to people about what I have read.
- ☐ I enjoy writing essays, diaries, articles and letters.
- ☑ I prefer listening to the radio or CDs to watching TV.
- ☑ I tend to hear words in my head before I speak or write them down.

My Score

Logical/Mathematical Intelligence

- ☐ New scientific developments fascinate me.
- ☐ I love Maths, Accounting and Science.
- ☐ I am interested in games like chess and bridge.
- ☐ I enjoy identifying patterns and logical sequences in things.
- ☐ I love to figure out how things work, e.g. my computer.
- ☐ Adding and subtracting numbers in my head is quite easy for me.
- ☑ I believe that almost everything has a rational and logical explanation.
- ☐ I get annoyed when other people are not being logical.
- ☐ I love to analyse things and put them into categories.
- ☐ I like to set up little 'what if' experiments.

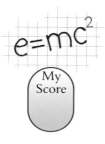

$e=mc^2$

My Score

Spatial/Visual Intelligence

- ☐ I can read maps quite easily.
- ☐ In Maths, I find geometry easier than algebra.
- ☑ My dreams are often vivid.
- ☑ I have strong opinions about which colours I like and don't like.
- ☑ I prefer books and magazines that have lots of pictures, images and diagrams.
- ☐ I love putting jigsaw puzzles together.
- ☑ I usually manage to find my way around places, even if I don't know them well.
- ☑ I love doodling when I am on the phone and I like to draw.
- ☐ I can visualise descriptions of things quite easily.
- ☑ I enjoy recording what I see by taking photos.

My Score

Kinaesthetic/Body Intelligence

- ☑ I like exciting physical experiences, e.g. bungee jumping.
- ☑ I prefer to learn by doing.
- ☐ I am involved in sport in my free time.
- ☐ I am good at craftwork, construction studies, woodwork or engineering.
- ☑ I find it hard to sit quietly for long periods of time.
- ☑ I need to touch and feel things to learn about them.
- ☐ I am well coordinated, i.e. I am not clumsy.
- ☑ I use my hands to gesticulate when I'm speaking.
- ☑ Good ideas often come to me when I am out walking or active in some way.
- ☐ I like to spend my free time outdoors when possible.

My Score

Musical Intelligence

- ☑ I often tap rhythmically while studying or working.
- ☑ I often find it difficult to stop humming a tune.
- ☑ Music plays an important role in my life.
- ☐ I am good at remembering melodies after hearing them once or twice.
- ☑ Without music, my life would lack something important.
- ☑ I am good at singing.
- ☑ I love having music in the background while I work.
- ☑ I know the tunes to lots of songs.
- ☑ I play a musical instrument or sing in a choir/band.
- ☑ I have a good ear for music and can identify if someone sings off key.

My Score

Interpersonal Intelligence

- ☑ I prefer group sports (e.g. hurling) to solo sports (e.g. running).
- ☑ I prefer social games/hobbies (e.g. drama) rather than ones that I do alone (e.g. reading).
- ☑ I enjoy sharing what I know with others.
- ☐ I am often the leader in activities.
- ☐ I find that people often ask me for advice.
- ☑ Crowds do not make me uncomfortable; I like being surrounded by people.
- ☑ I have a few close friends, not just one.
- ☐ I get involved in lots of activities connected with my school and the community.
- ☐ I am a member of several clubs.
- ☑ If I have a problem, I prefer to talk to others about it, instead of solving it by myself.

My Score

Intrapersonal Intelligence

- ☐ I like to keep a diary to reflect on my life.
- ☐ I have a hobby/interest that I pursue alone.
- ☐ Other people don't always share my opinions.
- ☑ I enjoy spending time alone.
- ☑ I am aware of my strengths and weaknesses.
- ☐ I enjoy meditation.
- ☑ I have goals/targets in my life that I think about often.
- ☑ I am strong-willed and don't mind if other people don't agree with me.
- ☑ I would love to run my own business rather than work for someone else.
- ☐ I like classes/magazine articles that help me to learn more about myself.

My Score

Naturalist Intelligence

- ☐ Environmental pollution bothers me and I am careful not to contribute to it.
- ☐ Biology is one of my favourite subjects.
- ☑ I recognise different models of car on the road.
- ☑ I love walking in the country or by the sea.
- ☑ I watch nature programmes on TV.
- ☑ When in the countryside I am very aware of nature and enjoy looking at plants, streams, rocks and flowers.
- ☐ I would like to work outside.
- ☐ I am interested in the names of the plants and trees around me.
- ☐ I like gardening.
- ☐ When eating or cooking, I think about the ingredients in the food and consider where they have come from and how they were grown.

My Score

(Adapted from a quiz in Thomas Armstrong's *Multiple Intelligences in the Classroom*.)

Results

The key to **multiple intelligences** is that once you have identified your strongest intelligence, you can use your strengths to support your weaknesses. For example, if you are verbally intelligent and have difficulties memorising pictures or images, you could try mentally labelling each part of a picture with a word to make remembering it easier. If, on the other hand, you are musically intelligent and have difficulty remembering dates, you can try memorising them as lyrics to a familiar tune or rap to aid your memory.

Your strongest intelligence represents the part of your brain that is most active and energetic. When you use that part, you are at your most focused and attentive; you understand and remember things much more easily. Use that intelligence to help support your weaker intelligences. Remember, that you will need to dedicate more time and energy to whatever intelligence you are weak in if you are to improve. For example, if you are weak linguistically, you can improve this intelligence by reading.

Nobody is strong in every intelligence. If you are weak in one, you'll find that you are strong in another. The important thing is to make the most of **your** strengths.

Using the **multiple intelligences fun quiz**, present your scores in the following chart.

	Linguistic	Logical	Kinaesthetic	Spatial	Musical	Interpersonal	Intrapersonal	Naturalist
10								
9					✓			
8								
7								
6			✓					
5	✓					✓	✓	
4				✓				✓
3								
2								
1		✓						

HIGHS	LOWS
My top 3 intelligences are …	What intelligences can I improve?
_____	_____
_____	_____
_____	_____

Aptitudes

These are your talents and abilities. Your Guidance Counsellor will usually give you different aptitude tests to help you to identify what you are good at. This type of testing may help you to find suitable careers that match your abilities.

Open Days

Attending open days is another way to research information on your career. Remember to plan open days using an Enterprise/Action Plan template if possible.

PLANNING YOUR CAREER INVESTIGATION

Success is rarely a matter of chance; it's usually the result of careful planning. You must realise the importance of planning. A plan is like a road map showing you where you are now, where you hope to get to and the route you have to take to reach your destination.

In planning your Career Investigation you must set yourself goals (whether they are personal or career goals). While planning, you should consider the following:

S	◎ Goals should be **Specific**.	Put pen to paper. Writing helps you to focus.
M	◎ Goals should be **Measurable**.	I hope to study or work at a particular subject so that I achieve a certain grade.
A	◎ Goals should be **Attainable**.	They should be achievable. Starting with short-term goals can make long-term goals easier to reach, e.g. instead of aiming to go from a D grade to a B, I may decide to go from a D3 to a D1 this term.
R	◎ Goals should be **Realistic**.	They should provide neither too great nor too small a challenge.
T	◎ Goals should have **Times** attached.	Allow yourself enough time to achieve the goal and to evaluate. Have you achieved what you wanted?

You must be **SMART** about your goals/aims when planning.

In the **Link Modules** you need to do the following:
- ○ Plan for yourself.
- ○ Understand and draft an Enterprise/Action Plan.
- ○ Understand and draft a business plan.

Portfolio Tip:
use an
Enterprise/Action
Plan template to
plan your career
investigation.

Remember you can submit An Enterprise/Action Plan on a Career Investigation as well as a Career Investigation, provided the Plan is not reproduced in the Investigation.

CROSS-CURRICULAR LINKS WITH LEAVING CERTIFICATE SUBJECTS

Remember it's important to relate your Leaving Certificate subjects, in particular your **V**ocational **S**ubject **G**roupings (**VSGs**), to work/career opportunities.

Careers associated with Languages

Lecturer

Teacher

LANGUAGES
All LCVP students
must have a
European language

Travel Agent

Translator

Identify other occupations related to European languages.

List your **V**ocational **S**ubject **G**roupings – (**VSGs**).

Possible Career Opportunities

Brainstorm possible career opportunities associated with your **V**ocational **S**ubject **G**roupings.

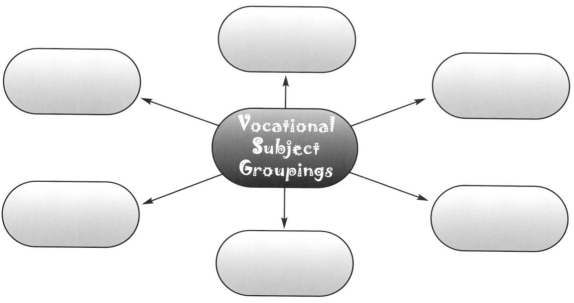

Vocational Subject Groupings

Careers and VSG Activity

My **V**ocational **S**ubject **G**rouping

[   ] **+** [   ]

Name **careers** that are directly linked to the study of [   ]

1.

2.

3.

Name **careers** that these subjects are compulsory for.

Subjects	**Careers**
1.	1.
2.	2.
3.	3.

Name **careers** where a **knowledge** of [   ] is useful.

1.

2.

3.

Can I study [   ] at **third level**? If yes, name 3 courses:

1.

2.

3.

Can I do a **work placement** (work experience/work shadow) related to
[   ]? If yes, name places:

1.

2.

3.

CAREER INVESTIGATION – INTERVIEW WITH A PERSON IN YOUR SELECTED CAREER

Some possible questions for a Career Investigation:

ENGINEERING
What does an engineer do?
List the different types of engineers.
What skills do you need to have to work in this area?
What qualities do you need?
What are the career prospects?
What are the different pathways to pursue a career in engineering?
Which pathway did you choose and why?
Which pathway would you recommend?
What qualifications and training are necessary?
Are those qualifications recognised internationally?
What salary does an engineer earn?
Traditionally, would this job have been considered a man's job or a woman's job?
What are the promotion prospects?
Do you enjoy your work?
What's the least interesting part of your work?
Others

Note: As part of your Career Investigation, you must interview and/or shadow a person in your selected career.

You may decide to design your own questionnaire depending on the career you are investigating.

WORK SHADOWING

As part of your Career Investigation you must participate in an **out-of-class learning experience**. One such activity may be a work shadow, and/or you may decide to participate in a work shadow as part of your work placement. Work shadowing provides you with an excellent opportunity to learn about careers of interest to you. Remember, in work shadowing you are **watching** rather than **doing**. It's also an excellent opportunity to improve your communication skills.

Portfolio Tip: Use the Enterprise/Action Plan template to plan your work shadow placement.

Planning and Preparing

Before starting your work shadow, you must plan carefully:
- ⚙ Generate a list of **questions** suitable to ask during a work shadow.
- ⚙ Explain the purpose of this experience to your employer. Describe the LCVP and your reasons for doing the work shadowing.
- ⚙ Document what you learn. Templates are an excellent way to do this.
- ⚙ Be aware of the **assessment criteria**. Consider the following carefully:
  - ▬ What are the **primary duties** and **responsibilities** of this job?
  - ▬ What **personal skills** and **characteristics** are required?
  - ▬ What kind of **career path** does this job have?
  - ▬ What **qualifications** and **training** are necessary?
  - ▬ What are the **rewards** and **frustrations** of this job?
  - ▬ What is the average **salary**?
  - ▬ Are **promotion prospects** good?
  - ▬ What **other information** do I require?

- ⚙ Be courteous at all times. Revise and follow safety, health and welfare regulations.
- ⚙ Allow yourself enough time to **reflect** and **evaluate** after your work shadow.
  - ▬ Record information.
  - ▬ Ask yourself if you now have all the information you need.
  - ▬ Ask yourself if you are suited to this career.
  - ▬ Think about what you have to do next.
  - ▬ Think about the skills you developed during the work shadow.

Link work shadowing with Unit 4 work placement.

After the work shadow, be sure to **thank** the employer. You may decide to do this by telephone, e-mail or by letter.

Finding a Work Shadow Placement

The following can prove useful in finding a work shadow placement:
- ⚙ Guidance Counsellor
- ⚙ Family, friends
- ⚙ Newspapers, magazines
- ⚙ Internet
- ⚙ Writing to or e-mailing an employer

Tip: Recap on job-seeking skills.

PORTFOLIO ITEM: CAREER INVESTIGATION REPORT

Things to keep in mind

* Compulsory: As part of your portfolio you must submit a total of **six** items. Your Career Investigation is part of the **mandatory** core.
* Your Career Investigation must be presented either as a word-processed document (300–600 words long) or as a 3–5-minute interview on cassette tape.
* You are encouraged to present material in a **logical** manner, using appropriate headings that enable you to fulfil the assessment criteria. The document should have a clear title and the name of the career should be displayed prominently.

> **Core**
> Submit all 4
> **Optional**
> Submit 2 out of 4
> A total of **6 portfolio items** must be submitted.

Assessment Criteria - Syllabus

The Career Investigation will assess your ability to:
* Generate a document with a clear and consistent layout.
* Describe a specific career concisely and accurately.
* Identify and categorise skills, qualities, qualifications and training relevant to the selected career.
* Describe two pathways to the selected career.
* Evaluate the selected career in the light of personal aptitudes, interests and choice of Leaving Certificate subjects.
* Present clear evidence of interaction with adults other than teachers in a relevant out-of-class learning experience.
* Evaluate the experience of undertaking a Career Investigation.

Career Investigation: Guidelines For Report Structure

1. **Title**: A clear title, i.e. Career Investigation and **name of career** being investigated should be displayed prominently.

2. **Description of Career**: This is a short outline of the type of work/duties that a person in the chosen career would be doing (2–3 sentences).

3. **Skills and Qualities**: List the skills and qualities that are relevant to the career.
   * List **3 skills**, for example, you need to know how to operate a machine to do this job.
   * List **3 qualities**, for example, to do this job you have to be good at dealing with the public. A quality describes the type of person you are.

4. **Qualifications and Training**
   You must outline **two pathways** to your selected job.
   * There may be two completely **different** pathways/routes to a career.
   * Where pathways are quite **similar**, outline them using the following:
     - Location
     - Course
     - Length of course and subjects
     - Entry requirements
     - Name of qualification
   * What if there is only **one definite route**? For example, there's only one way to join the Gardaí. In this case describe pathway one and your second pathway can be a contingency plan, e.g. what you will do while you're waiting to train. Will you do a PLC course in security studies?

5. **Out-of-Class Learning Experience**
   * You must name and date the activity.
   * Give a brief summary of what you learned about the career.
   * Activities may include:
     - Work shadow
     - Interview with a person in the career area
     - A careers exhibition or other events organised as part of the school's guidance programme

6. **Insights Gained**
   * Describe what insights you gained about the career as a result of your Career Investigation.
   * Describe what insights you gained about yourself as a result of the Career Investigation.

7. **Evaluation**
   * Discuss the career in light of your personal aptitudes, interests and choice of Leaving Certificate subjects.
   * Discuss the skills you developed as a result of the experience of undertaking the Career Investigation.

Career Investigation: Audio Interview Structure

You may opt to present this portfolio item in the form of an **audio cassette tape** on which you are interviewed for **3–5 minutes** about your Career Investigation.

A possible structure for such an interview, as outlined in **the NCCA Guidelines**, is given below:

1. **Would you like to introduce yourself?** Give your name and candidate number.

2. **You carried out a Career Investigation as part of your LCVP. What career did you choose to investigate?** Name the career.

3. **Why did you decide to investigate the career of ... ?** Mention your aptitudes, interests and choice of Leaving Certificate subjects.

4. **What exactly does a ... do?** Give a short description of the career.

5. **What skills and qualities would you need for a career in ...?** 'To be a ...one should have the ability to ....' (Mention at least three skills, e.g. the ability to operate machinery precisely, the ability to manage people etc.) 'And one should be the type of person who ...' (Mention three qualities, e.g. flexibility, an interest in people etc.)

6. **What training and qualifications would you need for this career?** Outline two pathways into the career (e.g. two courses you could do, education level/points required for entry, length of study/training, names of qualifications).

7. **What did you do outside the classroom to find out more about this career?** Describe and give date of work shadowing, interview with person in career area or visit to career related open day/exhibition.

8. **What do you think you learned from your Career Investigation?** Evaluate the selected career, e.g. 'I found I'm suited to this career because ...'. Evaluate the experience of doing a Career Investigation, e.g. 'I learned how to research'; 'I developed communication skills.'

> Remember, for the word-processed Career Investigation, the inclusion of materials downloaded directly from websites, software packages, or copied directly from other sources is not acceptable.

However, the inclusion of **specific requirements** downloaded from relevant websites or taken from publications is now permitted because the information is very specific and precise and is difficult to re-write accurately.

Resources

- ★ A Guidance Counsellor
- ★ Websites:
  - ▬ www.careerdirections.ie (database of all careers, A-Z)
  - ▬ www.qualifax.ie (database of courses)
  - ▬ www.cao.ie (courses and links to colleges)
  - ▬ www.vcas.com (courses in the UK)

Are there opportunities to pursue this career **locally, nationall**y and at an **international level**?

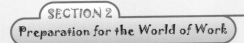

Career Investigation: Possible Template for Rough Work

Title: *Career Investigation of…*

Description of Career

> **Tip:** Use this template to record main points and key words. Revisit, elaborate on them and document them in your LCVP folder at a later stage. You may decide to start word-processing. Make sure you keep a back-up copy on your hard drive.

Skills and Qualities

Qualifications and Training
Pathway 1

Career Investigation: Possible Template for Rough Work

Pathway 2

Note: Make sure you are familiar with the required headings. They may be assessed in the written paper.

Interactions

Insights I Gained
   (a)   **About the career**

   (b)   **About myself**

Evaluation
   (a)   **Career**

   (b)   **Research**

An Outline of a Career Investigation Mind Map

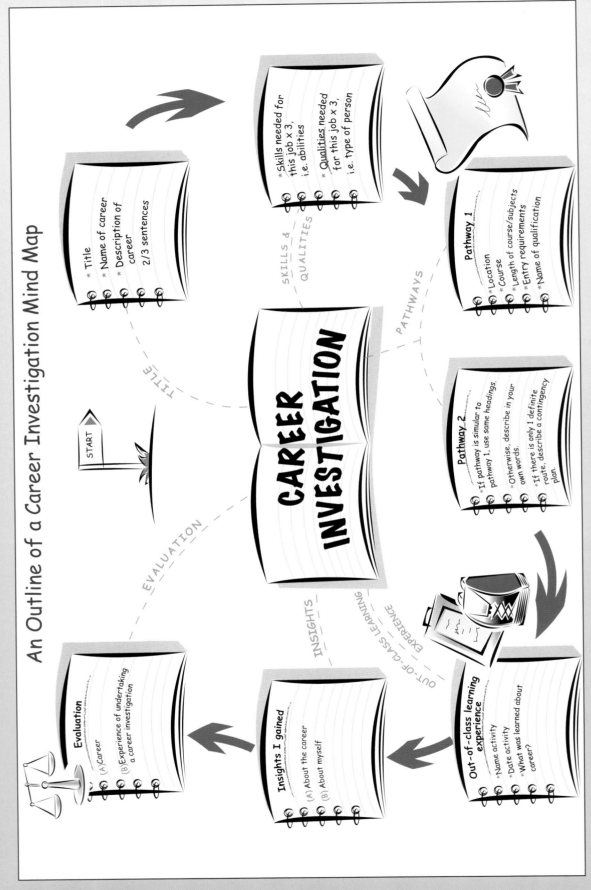

SAMPLE PORTFOLIO ITEM

CAREER INVESTIGATION

CAREER INVESTIGATION

Title: Career Investigation into Occupational Therapy

Author: Helen Shaughnessy

Summary
This investigation was undertaken in order to investigate the various routes and options available in the study of my chosen career.

Description of Career
Occupational Therapy involves 'helping people to help themselves'. An Occupational Therapist works with the individual to enhance the client's ability to perform daily tasks.

Skills and Qualities
I feel Occupational Therapists should be caring, patient and good communicators. Management and empathy are the skills I think one should have. I also think you need to be warm, friendly and have a liking for people, with good interpersonal skills, e.g. listening skills and the ability to be encouraging. I feel I possess all these characteristics. I come from a strong science background. I'm interested in medical science and I want to work in a profession that's caring and rewarding, and in which I'll work with people of all ages and types.

Findings
I learned that Occupational Therapy involves enabling individuals, groups and communities to develop the means and opportunities to identify, engage in and achieve their desired potential in their day-to-day activities.

Pathway 1
The first year of the Occupational Therapy Undergraduate Degree Programme lays down the foundations of the understanding and meaning of occupation to individuals and the relationship between occupation and health. Years two and three require students to develop knowledge of the occupational performance needs of particular groups of people. The final year will lean towards research, study and extended work placements. Further studies may also be achieved by completing a Doctoral or a Master of Science in Advanced Practice.

Entry Requirements
Access to Occupational Therapy is through the CAO system. Entry to this course requires a minimum Leaving Certificate grade of HC3 in a laboratory science subject and passes in four other subjects at H O level to include Irish, English, another language, Mathematics and one other subject. Last year's points were 490. I expect that a similar point level will be required this year as there is normally demand for this course.

CAREER INVESTIGATION

Pathway 2
My second pathway into Occupational Therapy is in the Robert Gordon University, Aberdeen, Scotland.

When studying Occupational Therapy at the Robert Gordon University an emphasis is placed on social and cultural aspects, as well as on current practice issues including ethical issues, research and communication practice. Throughout the first year, clinical sciences are introduced to provide an understanding of human function. Throughout the four years, there are various work placements with a particular emphasis on children and the disabled.

Entry Requirements
Entry to this course is based on an interview.

Interactions
Throughout my investigation I talked to my Guidance Counsellor. We discussed numerous aspects of Occupational Therapy and the different options that were available to me. I also interviewed Anne Dunne, an Occupational Therapist, on the 10th October 2004. She qualified in Scotland and gave me a great insight into both studying Occupational Therapy and the type of work involved.

Evaluation
Career (a)

In completing my career investigation I found that, although studying in Ireland would be more convenient, pathway two matched both my personality and my academic abilities. Pathway two in Scotland offers a more medical and science-based course and so meets more of my wants than pathway one. Scotland's focus on the science-based areas will prove more beneficial to me because I am studying Chemistry and Biology in my Leaving Certificate; they are my Vocational Subject Groupings for LCVP.

Research (b)

From my undertaking of my career investigation I gained invaluable information. It confirmed my decision to pursue Occupational Therapy as a career. The investigation improved my communication skills greatly because I interacted daily with my career guidance teacher and once a week with various medical professionals. My organisational skills also improved as I had to prepare and assemble the report. I now feel confident that I have the necessary skills to research a career.

SAMPLE PORTFOLIO ITEM

CAREER INVESTIGATION

Title: **CAREER INVESTIGATION**
A Career Investigation into Chartered Accountancy

Description of Accountancy:
Chartered Accountants provide professional financial services to businesses, such as auditing, financial analysis and advice on information systems and financial structures.

Skills
- You must have a high level of interpersonal skills and time organisational skills.
- You must be very motivated.

Qualities
- Accountants have to be innovative in solving problems which they encounter.
- Accountants must be hard-working and able to work under pressure to meet deadlines.
- Accountants must also be patient.

Interactions with Others
I interviewed Sarah Togher, a trainee accountant with Morris Accountants, Roscommon, on the 3rd March 2004. Sarah informed me of her training, salary and the difficulties involved in the work of an accountant. She also informed me of the different pathways to accountancy and explained that she opted for the direct entry route due to personal reasons. She offered me an opportunity to work shadow her in Morris Accountants. The work shadow was an ideal opportunity to research this career.

Pathway 1: The Direct Entry Pathway
- **Location**: School leavers enter into a training contract with a recognised training firm.
- **Length**: This contract lasts between 5 and 5.5 years.
- **Entry Requirements**: A minimum of 400 points in the Leaving Certificate and not lower than a C3 in Maths and English.
- **Qualifications**: When the training contract is over, if the trainee has passed the 3 professional exams and the final admitting exam, they become an associate member of the Institute of Chartered Accountants in Ireland (ICAI).

Pathway 2: The Graduate Route
- **Location**: Any candidate who has obtained a degree recognised by the ICAI can enter into a training contract with a recognised contract.
- **Length**: This is a 3.5-year contract.
- **Entry Requirements**: A recognised degree from a university or other third level institution.
- **Qualifications**: If they successfully complete the professional exams, they become an associate member of the ICAI.

Insights I Gained
- I now know a lot more about the work of an accountant and how to become a Chartered Accountant, including two pathways.
- From doing this Career Investigation and having participated in a Work Shadow, I now know that I would not be suited to a career in accountancy.

Evaluation
(a) **Career**
Personal Aptitudes, Interests and Leaving Certificate subjects:
- I felt that I would not like to pursue a career in accountancy because, although I possess many of the skills and qualities needed, I do not have accountancy as one of my Leaving Certificate subjects and I feel that I would not find the work interesting.

(b) **Researching a Career**
Skills Developed:
- I have learned how to research a certain career. I understand the information I researched and I can present it in a clear way.

LEARNING BOARD

Briefly summarise the main points using key words from the unit.	Something I **learned**...
_____ _____ _____ _____ _____ _____ _____ _____ _____ _____ _____	_____ _____ _____
	Something I found **difficult**...
	_____ _____ _____
	Write a short **Case Study** relating to a career you have researched.
	_____ _____ _____

DEVISE AN EXAM QUESTION

Start with a quotation, perhaps a **S**pecific **L**earning **O**utcome or a sentence from this unit.
_____
(a)
(b)
(c)

Write a **6-sentence presentation** on a work shadow placement.

_____
_____
_____
_____
_____
_____

LEARNING BOARD

Can I use this for my **portfolio**?   **Yes** ☐   **No** ☐
The portfolio is worth 60%.

If yes, tick the appropriate box below.

CORE – submit all 4
* Curriculum Vitae
* Career Investigation
* Summary Report
* Enterprise/Action Plan

OPTIONAL – submit 2 out of 4
* Diary of Work Experience
* Enterprise Report
* Recorded Interview/Presentation
* Report on 'My Own Place'

A total of 6 portfolio items must be submitted.

Now that you've worked through this unit, what are the next steps?

_____

_____

What new **skills** have I acquired?	Did I participate in any **teamwork** activities? If yes, specify.	Useful **websites**? www.careersworld.ie www.qualifax.ie Others…

Tasks
* Identify ways of researching a career.
* List five questions suitable to ask when interviewing a person about a selected career.
* Identify skills and qualities associated with the career you have investigated.
* Describe the contact you had with a person in your chosen career and the value of this contact for you.

CROSS-CURRICULAR

Cross-curricular learning refers to activities or themes which are relevant to many subjects across the curriculum, e.g. health and safety is important in Chemistry, Construction Studies, Engineering, Home Economics and Business.

* What Leaving Certificate subjects were useful? _____

_____

* How were they useful? _____

_____

* Were my **V**ocational **S**ubject **G**roupings useful?_____

_____

MAKING IT HAPPEN...
PREPARING FOR ASSESSMENT

**Assessment ideas based on Preparation for the World of Work
Unit 3 – Career Investigation**

Portfolio of coursework – 60%

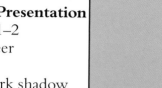

Core	Options
★ **Enterprise/Action Plan** - Plan a Career Investigation. - Plan a work shadow placement. ★ **Career Investigation**	★ **Recorded Interview/Presentation** (a) General interview, 1–2 questions on a Career Investigation (b) Presentation on work shadow placement, Career Investigation

Written Paper – 40%

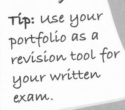

Tip: use your portfolio as a revision tool for your written exam.

*Revise the **layout** and **content of your portfolio items**.*

★ You may be assessed on the career you investigated, pathways, skills and qualities. Consider the following:
   - Personal skills
   - Technical skills
   - Interpersonal Skills
   - Opportunities to pursue a selected career locally, nationally and, where possible, at an international level
   - Interviews, **P**re-interview, **I**nterview and **P**ost-interview
   - Work shadow advantages, disadvantages, how to achieve a placement etc.
   - Teamwork
   - How personal targets are reached

★ Some questions may require that you demonstrate in your answer that you participated in a Career Investigation.
★ Cross-curricular learning – what Leaving Certificate subjects were useful and how? In particular, how were your **V**ocational **S**ubject **G**roupings useful?
★ Analyse your individual contribution and personal performance in this unit.
★ Evaluation involves looking at and judging the quality of an activity and asking yourself if you achieved your goals. Consider the following:
   - How and why do we evaluate?
   - How would you evaluate your suitability to the careers you researched?
   - Evaluate your Career Investigation.

SAMPLE EXAM QUESTIONS

These questions are mostly based on this unit only. In the written paper there may be questions which assess a few units together.

Q.1 You need to choose a career related to your aptitudes and interests.

(a) List a few careers you investigated during the LCVP. Describe one career in detail.

(b) List three skills and three qualities you have that make you suitable for this particular career.

(c) Identify the two Leaving Certificate subjects that you consider to be the most relevant to this career and explain why they are relevant.

(d) Describe how you went about investigating the career.

Q.2 A Career Investigation introduces you to the skills of career research and planning.

(a) As part of the LCVP, you must complete a Career Investigation. Present your findings as a one-page poster. Give at least five items of information.

(b) Draft a suitable personal statement highlighting your skills and qualities for the career you have investigated.

(c) Outline opportunities to pursue the career locally, nationally and, where possible, internationally.

(d) Describe the characteristics that employers look for in potential employees.

Q.3 A Career Investigation is a vital part of the LCVP.

(a) Describe the contact you had with a person from outside the school when investigating the career. How did you benefit from this contact?

(b) Outline how you would plan for a Career Investigation.

(c) Evaluation is an integral part of all LCVP activities. Comment on evaluation and evaluate your Career Investigation in three ways.

(d) List two personal skills, two technical/practical skills and two interpersonal skills for a career you have investigated.

Q.4 You have been asked to organise a career exhibition in your school.

(a) Draw up an agenda for a class meeting to organise the exhibition. Your agenda should contain at least six items.

(b) List categories of exhibitors who should be invited to attend.

(c) Draft a letter thanking exhibitors for their participation and explaining to them the benefits of a career exhibition, especially for LCVP students.

(d) Describe how you would evaluate this LCVP activity and explain the importance of evaluation.

Q.5 Planning is an essential part of your Career Investigation.

(a) Describe ways in which participation in the LCVP may improve your career opportunities.

(b) List what a personal profile can contain.

(c) Discuss the importance of open days and explain how they benefit LCVP students.

(d) Comment on the importance of planning your Career Investigation.

LINK MODULE 1 – PREPARATION FOR THE WORLD OF WORK

UNIT 4 – WORK PLACEMENT

In this unit, you are encouraged to plan, organise and engage in a **work placement** (work experience/work shadowing). If possible, the placement should be consistent with your career aspirations. This will give you practical experience of an adult working environment, as well as helping you to develop your organisational and communicative skills. The unit should conclude with a debriefing session, where you are encouraged to reflect on and evaluate your experiences.

.

SPECIFIC LEARNING OUTCOMES – SLOs

(as listed in the syllabus)

When you have finished working through this unit, you should be able to:

4.1	specify personal goals in relation to a work placement
4.2	plan and organise a work placement
4.3	attend punctually for a specific placement
4.4	dress appropriately for a specific placement
4.5	follow a set of procedures in accordance with specific instructions
4.6	communicate effectively with other workers in a particular placement
4.7	follow a specific set of instructions relating to Health and Safety
4.8	review personal experiences in relation to a work placement
4.9	analyse reports by adults of personal performance in a workplace
4.10	reflect on and evaluate a specific work placement in the light of career aspirations
4.11	describe how what has been learned can be applied to work at home, in school and in the community
4.12	present a diary/written/verbal report on a specific work placement
4.13	link the activities in this unit to learning in relevant Leaving Certificate subjects

The work placement is a key component of the LCVP. From a learning perspective, work placements are a very powerful activity. You might only engage in a limited amount of work but you can learn a lot by observing, interacting and communicating with adults in the workplace. It's an ideal opportunity to explore your career aspirations and interests, while also learning from debriefing, reflection and evaluation.

It's also an opportunity to try out your job-seeking skills from Unit 2, as well as other skills acquired during the LCVP. The minimum time you should be involved in work-related activities outside the school is **five days**.

You may decide to do a work shadow along with other out-of-school, work-related activities, e.g. a 2-day work shadow, a visit to FÁS, an interview with a person in your selected career and attendance at a college open day. If you decide to opt for a work shadow, one of the daily entries may be about preparation for the work shadow or it may be possible to engage in a **5-day work experience**.

You're encouraged to find your own placement and it's important to look upon the placement as an educational activity and not to expect payment.

A work placement can be seen as giving you a real taste of the world of work. The more prepared you are, the more worthwhile the work placement will be.

Note: A **5-day** work experience will ensure lots of content for your Diary.

As with all LCVP activities, much time is given to the **learning cycle**. The learning cycle consists of five steps: plan, activity, debrief, evaluate and record. **PEP** (**P**re-experience, **E**xperience and **P**ost-experience) incorporates all of these steps.

PLAN	PRE-EXPERIENCE
ACTIVITY	EXPERIENCE
DEBRIEF EVALUATE RECORD	POST-EXPERIENCE

Your work placement (work experience/work shadow) is an opportunity to gain valuable experience in the real world of work.

A work placement can help me to …

_____

_____

_____

WORK PLACEMENT: WORK SHADOWING OR WORK EXPERIENCE

As part of this module each student is expected to engage in a work placement, either work experience or work shadowing. Ideally the work placement should be consistent with your career aspirations.

Work Experience

This involves gaining experience in a particular work environment by carrying out particular tasks and engaging in duties associated with that type of work.

Advantages

- ⚙ This type of placement offers an insight into the duties, tasks and responsibilities associated with a particular type of work.
- ⚙ This experience can relate directly to your career aspirations.
- ⚙ During the work experience you can make contacts for future work, get content for your CV, and acquire referees.
- ⚙ This type of experience will help you to develop and improve interpersonal, communication and organisational skills.
- ⚙ Experiencing a placement can motivate you to work harder on returning to school.
- ⚙ You will have the chance to interact with adults other than teachers and parents.
- ⚙ This experience should be viewed as an opportunity to learn new skills, e.g. teamwork skills, and to acquire new knowledge, e.g. regarding health and safety regulations. You will then be able to use these skills and knowledge at home, at school and in the community.

Portfolio Tip: Use Enterprise/Action Plan template to plan work placement.

Tip: Revise job-seeking skills.

Work Shadowing

Work shadowing is an alternative to work experience and may also be an option for the Career Investigation. In work shadowing your role is to **observe** a working environment and the people in it, rather than to engage in tasks. It allows you to learn about a job by **watching**. Work shadowing doesn't usually last as long as work experience.

Advantages

- ⚙ You can expose yourself to a variety of careers by doing a couple of shorter placements.
- ⚙ This type of placement helps to improve interpersonal and communication skills: you have to ask questions, which in turn helps interview skills.
- ⚙ Work shadowing is particularly suitable for careers that don't lend themselves to work experience, e.g. social work.
- ⚙ During the placement, you can make contacts for future work, get content for your CV and acquire referees.
- ⚙ Since work shadowing placements are shorter, they can be arranged throughout the year and are less disruptive to schools.
- ⚙ You may also be encouraged to sample careers a little bit beyond your reach.
- ⚙ You can see the world of work and experience the transition from school to work.
- ⚙ Experiencing a placement can motivate you to work harder.
- ⚙ You will have the chance to interact with adults other than teachers and parents.

Revise rights and responsibilities and legislation (Unit 1) and interview skills (Unit 2).

PREPARING FOR MY WORK PLACEMENT

Pre-placement

- ❖ Set your objectives.
- ❖ Develop organisational and communication skills.
- ❖ Brief employers and parents.
- ❖ Prepare a CV.
- ❖ Revise letter writing and write a letter.
- ❖ Revise telephoning/e-mail.
- ❖ Revise interview techniques.
- ❖ Organise transport.
- ❖ Inform your principal.
- ❖ Get insurance forms.
- ❖ Get employers' report forms (see p. 121).

Tip: Revise Job-seeking Skills (Unit 2).

During the Placement

- ❖ Find out about the company.
- ❖ Make a note of your duties.
- ❖ Make a note of training.
- ❖ Write down your observations.
- ❖ Make a note of interactions with staff.
- ❖ Describe the dress code.
- ❖ Describe a typical day.
- ❖ Describe your highs.
- ❖ Describe your lows.
- ❖ Make a note of safety, health and welfare regulations.
- ❖ Note other relevant **SLOs.**

Tip:
Document learning **each day,** using templates. Record main points.

Post-placement

- ❖ What did I learn about the job?
- ❖ What skills are required to do this job?
- ❖ What qualities are required to do this job?
- ❖ Am I suitable?
- ❖ How can I improve?
- ❖ How did I overcome problems?
- ❖ How did I master unfamiliar tasks?
- ❖ What knowledge and skills can I apply at home, at school and in the community?
- ❖ Are there any career possibilities?
- ❖ Did I make contacts for the future?
- ❖ What would I do differently?
- ❖ Would I recommend the job to others?
- ❖ Send a thank-you message to the employer by letter or by e-mail.
- ❖ From the templates, prepare a Diary of Work Experience.

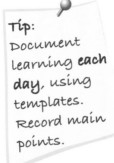

Participating in a work placement is an ideal opportunity to practise and improve **communication skills.**

LEARNING OPPORTUNITIES

The work placement is an ideal opportunity to learn new skills and to apply LCVP **SLOs**, that is to apply the skills you have acquired while studying the LCVP.

Communications

Communication is the transfer of information from one person to another. A good communicator ensures that information is correctly **given**, **received** and **understood**. Ways of improving your communications skills include:

* **Practise speaking in public:** This will help you with tone and speed and will help you overcome any feelings of nervousness.
* **Know your subject:** You will come across as more confident and relaxed.
* **Learn to listen carefully:** Listening skills help you to understand and avoid being distracted. Remember we have 'two ears and one mouth'!
* **Do a communications course:** This will highlight what you need to improve.
* **Join a club, preferably as an officer (chairperson, secretary, treasurer):** You will be able to practise communicating.
* **Learn to improve your body language:** Practise in front of a mirror.
* **Practise writing reports/letters:** Ensure that you use appropriate language and make sure the content and layout are clear.

Sharon Ní Bheoláin
is an example of a
good communicator.

Importance of Communication Skills

* Good communication means that what you say is accurate, comprehensible (easily understood) and appropriate.
* The ability to communicate well creates a good impression, e.g. with customers.
* Remember, communication skills are a characteristic of entrepreneurs, a desirable quality for employees and a necessary quality for leaders.

Listening as a Communication Skill

DO	DON'T
⚙ Show interest	⚙ Pass judgement
⚙ Encourage	⚙ Interrupt
⚙ Empathise	⚙ Day-dream
⚙ Ask the person to clarify if you don't understand	⚙ Argue or jump to conclusions

Identify a good communicator.

_____

Why is he/she good at communicating?

_____

Health and Safety in the Workplace

Don't forget the Safety, Health and Welfare at Work Act. During your work placement you must be able to follow instructions relating to the Act. Remember too that both employers and employees have obligations. Employees' obligations include the following:

- You should follow instructions and heed training.
- You should use protective equipment.
- You should report any dangers or injuries.
- You should use all equipment in the proper manner.
- You should not endanger others.
- You should look out for safety signs.
- You should ask your employer for their safety statement.
- You should give your insurance details to your employer.
- If harassed or bullied, inform your contact person and school.

If for some reason you can't attend your work placement, notify your contact person immediately. Don't forget to inform your school.

Tip: Revise legislation from Unit 1.

Note: This may be a question in the written exam.

EVALUATING YOUR WORK PLACEMENT

Remember the importance of **evaluation**.

In what ways can your work placement be evaluated?

- Your work placement can be evaluated by the quality and content of your Diary of Work Experience, in particular the evaluation.
- It can be evaluated by getting the employer to complete an evaluation form or by interviewing the employer.
- It can be evaluated by assessing your progress in school after the placement. Maybe you're more motivated and working harder. You can ask your teachers to comment.
- Class discussions on what you have learned and how your skills have improved can also be used as a method of evaluating the work placement.

Identify **suitable headings** for a brief evaluation.

What I learned: _____

What I liked: _____

What I disliked: _____

Views on my career choice: _____

Skills used: _____

Value of work placement: _____

*Note: You may be asked to identify **headings** for evaluating your work placement in the written exam.*

Work Placement – a Guide to Evaluation

Using the following rating scale, please mark the relevant box:

Strongly Disagree	Disagree	Unsure	Agree	Strongly Agree
1	2	3	4	5

RATING SCALE

1. I was punctual during the placement.
   1   2   3   4   5

2. I dressed appropriately.
   1   2   3   4   5

3. I was able to follow a set of procedures.
   1   2   3   4   5

4. I improved my communications skills.
   1   2   3   4   5

5. I showed initiative.
   1   2   3   4   5

6. I was reliable.
   1   2   3   4   5

7. I overcame challenges.
   1   2   3   4   5

8. I interacted with staff/volunteers.
   1   2   3   4   5

9. I showed progression from the first to the final day.
   1   2   3   4   5

10. I participated well in teamwork.
   1   2   3   4   5

11. I improved my skills.
   1   2   3   4   5

12. I improved my knowledge.
   1   2   3   4   5

Tip: After completing this evaluation, write a brief account of evaluation in my work placement.

How can you evaluate your work placement?

13. I mastered unfamiliar tasks.

  ☐1   ☐2   ☐3   ☐4   ☐5

14. I applied what I learned to work at school/home and in the community.

  ☐1   ☐2   ☐3   ☐4   ☐5

15. I learned more about legislation.

  ☐1   ☐2   ☐3   ☐4   ☐5

16. I improved my researching skills.

  ☐1   ☐2   ☐3   ☐4   ☐5

17. I became more confident.

  ☐1   ☐2   ☐3   ☐4   ☐5

18. I became more organised.

  ☐1   ☐2   ☐3   ☐4   ☐5

19. I am now more familiar with career options in this area.

  ☐1   ☐2   ☐3   ☐4   ☐5

20. I am more aware of my suitability to this type of work.

  ☐1   ☐2   ☐3   ☐4   ☐5

Remember, this may be a question in the written paper.

Total Score ☐ **Maximum 100**

The higher the score, the more you have achieved from your work placement. Are there any areas for improvement?

_____

_____

MY HIGHS	MY LOWS
My top 3 achievements were:	What can I improve on?

EMPLOYER'S REPORT ON LCVP WORK PLACEMENT

Employer's name and address:

_____

_____

Student's Name:

Attendance Date/s: No. of Days:

Please tick the following (✓)

	Excellent	Acceptable	Poor	Please Comment
Time-keeping				
Relationship with others				
Initiative				
Ability to carry out tasks				
Ability to follow instructions				
Ability to overcome problems				
Attitude towards job				

Any additional information:

_____

_____

_____

_____

Signed: _____

Position: _____ Date: _____

Many thanks for your help with our work placement programme.

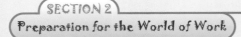

PORTFOLIO ITEM: DIARY OF WORK EXPERIENCE

The **Diary of Work Experience** is an outcome of Unit 4 of Preparation for the World of Work. The diary may be submitted by you if you have participated in a traditional work experience placement or engaged in work shadowing.

When preparing for the Diary of Work Experience, you should be guided by the **S**pecific **L**earning **O**utcomes related to work placements and, if possible, you should also use the experience as an opportunity to gain knowledge for other **S**pecific **L**earning **O**utcomes from the syllabus, perhaps from the enterprise module.

Things to keep in mind

* ★ Optional: As part of your portfolio you must present a total of **six** items. The Diary of Work Experience is part of the **optional** items.
* ★ Your diary can be presented as a word-processed or handwritten document (1,000–1,500 words long).
* ★ Begin with an introduction page.
* ★ Ensure that the document has a clear diary structure.
* ★ Include a minimum of three dated entries and a maximum of five.
* ★ Allow one page per dated entry.

Assessment Criteria - Syllabus

The Diary of Work Experience will assess your ability to:
* ★ Generate a document with a clear and consistent layout.
* ★ Name and give a concise description of the work experience placement.
* ★ Provide an explanation of why the placement was selected.
* ★ Give a sequential day-to-day account of the experience.
* ★ Analyse personal performance.
* ★ Evaluate the experience in light of personal vocational aspirations.
* ★ Apply what has been learned to work at home, at school and in the community.

Diary of Work Experience: Guidelines for Structure

1. **Introductory Page**
   * A clear title stating that this is a Diary of Work Experience must be included.
   * Author's name, i.e. your name, should be included.
   * Name and address of employer
   * Dates: specify the dates of your work placement.
   * Title of job: indicate the position that you were investigating or doing work experience in.
   * Job description: give a brief summary of your duties.
   * Why I selected this work placement:
     - Ideally, the placement should be consistent with your career aspirations or interests. You should mention your aptitudes and interests, the Leaving Certificate points that would be required to gain entry to a course to train for this job and your choice of Leaving Certificate subjects.
     - You can also refer to knowledge, skills and experience you hope to gain through the placement.

2. **Three to five daily entries**, clearly dated. **One page per day** is recommended. Each daily entry can be structured like the example below:

Day 1, 2, 3, 4 or 5 Starting Time:	Date: Finishing Time:
Duties Performed **Training** **Interactions with staff/customers** **Observations** **Problems** **Mastered Unfamiliar Tasks** **Others Viewed your Performance** **Evaluation**	

3. **Evaluation**
   * Consider your **suitability** to the particular organisation and working environment.
   * Research **career possibilities** in the area that you have done your work experience.
   * Consider the relevance of **skills** gained and **contacts** made to future career goals.

4. **Application**
   How would you apply **both** the **knowledge** (e.g. health and safety) and **skills** (e.g. communication skills) gained through the placement to each of the following areas – **home, school and the community**? Write a short paragraph or a bulleted list.

   Note: Don't forget to apply **both** knowledge and skills.

5. **Appendices**
   Maximum of **two** items may be included.

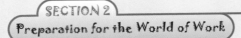
Diary of Work Experience: Possible Template for Rough Work

DIARY OF WORK EXPERIENCE

Student Name:

Name and Address of Employer:

Dates of Work Experience:

Title of Job:

Job Description

Why I Selected this Work Placement

Tip: It should be consistent with your **career** aspirations.

DIARY OF WORK EXPERIENCE

Day: One   Starting Time:
Date: Finishing Time:

Duties Performed

Training

Portfolio Tip: Follow the important guidelines on p. **123** to get the content requirements of each of the headings.

Instructions

Interactions with Staff/Customers

Observations

Problems

Mastered Unfamiliar Tasks

My Perception of How Others Viewed my Performance

Evaluation of Today

DIARY OF WORK EXPERIENCE

Day:	*Two*	Starting Time:
Date:		Finishing Time:

Duties Performed

Training

Remember the diary may be word-processed or handwritten.

Instructions

Interactions with Staff/Customers

Observations

Problems

Mastered Unfamiliar Tasks

My Perception of How Others Viewed my Performance

Evaluation of Today

DIARY OF WORK EXPERIENCE

Day: *Three*   **Starting Time:**

Date: **Finishing Time:**

Duties Performed

Training

Instructions

You may decide to use this template with word-processed headings and handwrite the remainder. If so, ensure you have good handwriting.

Interactions with Staff/Customers

Observations

Problems

Mastered Unfamiliar Tasks

My Perception of How Others Viewed my Performance

Evaluation of Today

DIARY OF WORK EXPERIENCE

Day: *Four*   Starting Time:
Date: Finishing Time:

Duties Performed

Training

Instructions

Interactions with Staff/Customers

Observations

Problems

Mastered Unfamiliar Tasks

My Perception of How Others Viewed my Performance

Evaluation of Today

DIARY OF WORK EXPERIENCE

Day:	*Five*	Starting Time:
Date:		Finishing Time:

Duties Performed

Training

Instructions

Interactions with Staff/Customers

Observations

Problems

Mastered Unfamiliar Tasks

My Perception of How Others Viewed my Performance

Evaluation of Today

DIARY OF WORK EXPERIENCE

Evaluation

Tip: Use the following headings: Suitability, Career Possibilities, Skills Gained and Contacts Made.

Application

Tip: Apply **skills** and **knowledge** to work at home, at school and in the community.

An Outline of a Diary of Work Experience Mind Map

START

TITLE PAGE

* Title
* Name & Address of Employer
* Dates
* Title of Job
* Brief Job Description Why I selected this work placement

DATED ENTRIES

SHOW PROGRESSION

Day 5
Day 4
Day 3
Day 2

Day 1   **Date**
* Starting Time/Finishing Time
* Duties performed
* Training
* Instructions
* Observations
* Problems
* Master unfamiliar Tasks
* How others viewed you

Diary of Work Experience

APPENDICES

Appendices

Maximum of two items

APPLICATION

Application
* How will you apply knowledge and skills at home, in school and in the community?

EVALUATION

Evaluation
* Suitability
* Career Possibilities
* Relevant skills gained and contacts made

SAMPLE PORTFOLIO ITEM

DIARY OF WORK EXPERIENCE

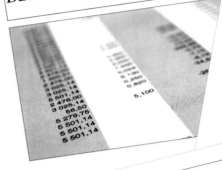

DIARY OF WORK EXPERIENCE

Name:
Name and address of employer:

Peter Broderick
Mr. Fergal Giblin,
Owner and manager,
Swan Accountants,
High Street,
Tralee, Co. Kerry.

Dates of work experience: 27th – 30th October 2005
Position: Office Assistant

Duties
- Collecting and filing customer files, including audit and tax files.
- Typing out letters and adding figures using computers.
- Photocopying documents.
- Adjusting accounts.
- Adding up cashbooks and comparing them to accounts on computers.

Reasons why I selected this work experience
I selected this work experience because I am presently taking business as one of my Leaving Certificate subjects and I am considering doing a Business Degree in college. Chartered accountancy is one of the many areas in which a business graduate can work. I felt that working in an accountant's office would give me a valuable insight into what an accountant's work ...

Day 2: Tuesday
Date: 28th October 2005

Starting Time: 8.55 a.m.
Finishing Time: 17.15 p.m.

Duties Performed
- Filing tax and audit files.
- Photocopying various documents for people in the office.
- Adding up cashbooks.

Training
I was shown the filing system that is used for the hard copy of all the customers' tax and audit files for the firm. I was then given some customer files, which needed to be put away in the filing room upstairs.
After I had the filing completed, I was shown how to use the photocopier. I then had to photocopy various documents for different people in the office.
... the afternoon, I was shown how to add up cashbooks and compare the figures I got to the figures on the ... uter files.

...tion
... to know a lot more of the staff. Many of the staff are trainee accountants, and I found that they ... ed to have someone to take care of the small jobs like photocopying and adding up cashbooks

...rmance
... more challenging than yesterday because I was delegated a lot more responsibility, but I ... e to cope well with this.

... the trainee accountants in the firm are given a lot more of the basic and time-
... g up cashbooks and checking their figures against those on the computer.

... cashbooks difficult because it took a long time to get the figures to match

---

Starting Time: 8.55 a.m.
Finishing Time: 17.15 p.m.

Day 1: Monday
Date: 27th October 2005

Duties Performed
- Basic accountancy using computers.
- General office work.

Training
I was shown the basics of using the accountancy programme on the computer and the basics of Microsoft Excel. I then tried some simple problems given to me by the other workers. Once I had completed these and I was a little more comfortable using the programmes, I had more figures to input into the computer and then I had to add these up with the existing accounts.

Daily Performance
I was a little nervous when I first entered the office. After I was introduced to everybody and shown what to do, I became more relaxed. I enjoyed working on the computer and it really helped me to settle in.

Observations
I noticed that there was a more relaxed atmosphere in the office than I had expected. People were laughing and joking with each other, but still getting their work done.

Problems
When I first started using the accountancy programme on the computer, I found it a little hard to get used to, but after some practice my confidence grew and I now wish to learn more about the programme.

SAMPLE PORTFOLIO ITEM

Day 3: Wednesday
Date: 29th October 2005

Starting Time: 9.00 a.m.
Finishing Time: 17.20 p.m.

Duties Performed
- Photocopying.
- Arranging photocopied documents and filing them away.
- Filling out schedule forms for cash payment invoices.

Training
I already knew how to use the photocopier and how to file away all the documents I duplicated, therefore I didn't need any extra training in this area. In the afternoon, I was shown how to fill out schedule forms for cash payment invoices. This was a simple enough task and it was similar to what I had been doing the last couple of days.

Daily Performance
I found that I felt as if I had settled in today. I am getting to know a lot more of the employees and I had no problems finding my way around the offices. I didn't find the work as challenging today because of what I had been doing the previous two days.

Observations
Today I was working with one of the qualified chartered accountants. He told me a lot about his work and how long it took him to become qualified. I found from talking to him that he finds the work very repetitive and boring and that the main reason he became an accountant is because it is a secure job and once you qualified the pay is good.

I hope to interview David McGrath, a qualified accountant, in detail for my Career Investigation.

Day 4: Thursday
Date: 30th October 2005

Starting Time: 8.55 a.m.
Finishing Time: 17.30 p.m.

Duties Performed
- Filing tax and audit files.
- Photocopying documents that were to be added to each customer file I was then putting away.

Instructions
I was given sole responsibility for filing away all tax and audit files when the other employees were finished with them. I also had to photocopy various documents and add them to each file as I was putting them away.

Interaction
I was working with all members of the office today. They were all glad to have somebody to help them today because Thursday is usually the busiest day of the week.

Daily Performance
I was working under a lot more pressure today and I enjoyed the amount of responsibility I had. I felt I coped well with the pressure of meeting the deadlines, and I found that I was a bigger part of the team today because I helped them to meet their deadlines. I enjoyed the team approach.

Observations
Even though it was a lot busier in the office, the atmosphere did not change from the previous three days. I did find that the managers were a little harder on the trainee accountants today, but this is all part of their training and getting them used to working under pressure.

Problems
I did not experience any problems with the work I had to do today because I had got used to doing it over the last three days. I did find working under pressure to meet deadlines a little harder today but I got used to it.

Evaluation
From doing this work experience in Swan Accountants I learned a lot more about the work a chartered accountant has to do. I found that the work can become very repetitive and monotonous and, although I did not mind this for the short term, I do not know if I would like it as a career, although I did enjoy doing the work while I was there.

From spending the four days working in an office environment I learned what the atmosphere can be like, and it was a little different than I had expected. Most times in the office there was a very relaxed atmosphere. As long as the work got done everybody was happy, but when things got busier, the managers began to give more orders and the atmosphere changed. I do not think I would enjoy working from an office all the time because of this; also it can become very confined.

Overall, working in Swan Accountants was a rewarding experience because I got to experience life in the working world. I also learned that they provide a direct-entry school-leavers training course there and that if I do choose to pursue a career in accountancy, this would be a good route to take.

Application
From working in the accountants' office I have learned many skills, which have helped both in business class and in LCVP. I learned many of the terms, which are associated with business and I now have a better understanding of business as a subject. I also learned some basic accountancy while working there. This has made the accounting section of the business course a lot easier for me and it has also helped me a lot when doing the accounts for my reports for LCVP. This is something I can also apply at home, at school and in the community.

While working in Swan Accountants, a lot of the time I had to work unsupervised. Doing this has greatly improved my organisational skills, both at home and at school. I am now better able to organise my homework and study timetables and I am much better at motivating myself to get all my work complete. I also gained a lot of knowledge, which will be of value to me even in my local community.

SAMPLE PORTFOLIO ITEM

DIARY OF WORK EXPERIENCE

Starting Time:	9.00 a.m.
Finishing Time:	12.30 p.m.

Day 1: Monday
Date: 27th October 2005

Duties Performed
- Observing each child.
- Organising lunch-time.
- Preparing each child for home time.

Training
On my first day, I received a little training before the children arrived. The leader, Josephine, explained the rules of the Montessori school to me. She outlined simple safety procedures that must be followed by each staff member and the children themselves. She also explained the rules that were laid down for the children and how to deal with problems if they arise.

Daily Performance
It was my first day and I was really nervous, but I soon settled into things when I met Josephine and the children. After the children arrived, Josephine introduced me to the class. My first task for the day was to sit on a chair in the corner and observe the children from a distance. I sat there for two hours and in that time I got to know the personalities and temperaments of the children as they played. At lunch-time I handed out the biscuits and drinks and then helped clean up the school. Before home time I read the children a story in a circle. I did this as an exercise both for me and for them. I felt at the end of the first day that both the children and I were more at ease with each other and ready for the next day.

Observation
After my first day I was a lot more relaxed. I felt a lot more at ease with the staff and the children and was looking forward to the next day. I felt that I didn't have much interaction with the children today; however Josephine said that on Tuesday I was going to have to do a lot more and today was only an introduction.

Problems I encountered
On my first day I was nervous but I relaxed as the day went on because everyone was friendly and helpful. I found the day really challenging and different to what I was used to. Getting to know the children's names and temperaments also proved to be challenging. I also found that getting the children's full attention was difficult and I had to resort to forming a circle for reading time, which proved to be successful.

DIARY OF WORK EXPERIENCE

Title: Diary of Work Experience

Name: Mary Carragher

Name and Address of Employer: Josephine Williams,
Main Street,
Letterkenny,
Co. Donegal

Dates: 27th October – 29th October 2005

Position: Assistant carer and teacher in a Montessori school

Duties
- Organising daily projects for each individual child.
- Organising lunch- and play-time.
- Preparing the children for home time.
- Tidying the school after lunch.
- Watching and observing the children's daily tasks.

Reasons why I selected this work experience
I selected my work experience in a Montessori school because I wanted to gain experience working with young children. I felt that having a designated time with a class full of children would prepare me for any other career involving children, e.g. paediatric nursing or primary school teaching. I thought it would test my communication skills, my understanding of children and my patience to the utmost.

SAMPLE PORTFOLIO ITEM

| Day 2: | Tuesday | Starting Time: | 9.00 a.m. |
| Date: | 28th October 2005 | Finishing Time: | 12.30 p.m. |

Duties Performed
- I organised an art project incorporating the theme of families.
- I listened to the children counting and reciting the alphabet.
- I prepared songs to sing in circle time.

Daily Performance
I felt a lot more comfortable as it was my second day and I was getting used to the children in the class. I had lots of preparation to do for the art project. I then called each child up one at a time to my desk. This gave me time alone with them to get to know them. I then listened to each child count and recite the alph bet. It was soon time for home, so I formed a circle and we sang the songs which I had prepared. I waite with the children until they were collected and then helped clean up the room.

Observation
After the day I had gained more confidence with the children than I had with them the previous day beginning to get used to the Montessori school and I was learning fast. I found that the more time I spending with them, the closer they became to me. I also observed that each child had very differe I also found that they were really interested in the song circle and were really hyper and active.

| Day 3: | Wednesday | Starting Time: | 9.00 a.m. |
| Date: | 29th October 2005 | Finishing Time: | 12.30 p.m. |

Duties Performed
- Assisting the class with their preparations for their variety show.
- Organising home time.
- Helping with lunch- and play- time.

Daily Performance
Today was my last day and I was really disappointed as I was only getting to know each child. However I still had the day and wanted to enjoy it as much as possible. Firstly I had to help out with the variety show practice. The children were putting on this little show for their parents next month. I loved seeing them sing and dance. They were so adorable. It was so much fun to see them practise and I loved helping them. Today I also helped with lunch and played with the children in the garden. At the end of the day, I thanked Josephine and the other carers and said good-bye to each child as they left. Finally I organised home time for their help and advice.

Observation
Today's experience was brilliant. I really saw the children's personalities shine when they were practising for the show. It was really rewarding helping them. Saying good-bye was really sad but as they went, I got satisfaction from knowing that I had helped them over the last few days.

Evaluation
I felt sad that my experience was finished. I would have loved to have stayed for a few more days. Overall it was a really enjoyable experience and I would love to do it again. I gained invaluable experience from my work experience and felt that it was a great help to me for my future career choices.

I found my work experience in the Montessori school very rewarding and interesting. It exceeded all my expectations of what I had thought previous to my work experience. The insight I got by being there was incredible. It made me re-evaluate some of the courses and careers that I had been considering. Each day made me feel good about myself and I got satisfaction that I had helped so many young people during the day. It was really meaningful work and I learned a lot from it. However, I have learned that it is a very demanding and intense career, but the rewards that you get are worth it. I enjoyed the week immensely and feel I was very suited to a career in the caring for children. It is an area which I am definitely pursuing, and all of my CAO choices are based within this field. I feel that having the opportunity to go on a week's work experience to the Montessori school really opened my eyes to the area I am pursuing.

Application
I have gained various skills and knowledge as a result of my work experience in the Montessori school:
- As a result of my work experience the main knowledge I gained was that I enjoyed working with children. I realised that I want to work with people in the future as I find it very satisfying and rewarding. I feel that this has helped with my babysitting at home and in the community. In school it has helped me deal with the younger students.
- I feel I have also improved my leadership skills as a result of my work experience. I now feel that after my work experience I can take control of situations: at home, guiding my younger siblings; in school with an area dealing with young children, as one has to lead by example. This is essential in Montessori students in the years below me; and in the community with the younger generation.
- I have also improved my ability to motivate and motivate the child to learn and develop their self-esteem. I have adapted this new skill at school with class work and at home with my studies. I have also applied it to the community by taking part in our local Meals on Wheels Organisation and motivating others to do so too.
- I also learned that communication is the essential key when dealing with children. Without good communication in this area, healthy student and teacher relationships would not exist. I feel this skill has helped me immensely in school with my own teachers, at home with my family and in the community with my friends.

LEARNING BOARD

Briefly summarise the main points using key words from the unit.	Something I **learned**...
	Something I found **difficult**...
	Write a short **Case Study** relating to your work placement.

DEVISE AN EXAM QUESTION

Start with a quotation, perhaps a **S**pecific **L**earning **O**utcome or a sentence from this unit.

(a)

(b)

(c)

Write a **6-sentence presentation** on communications.

LEARNING BOARD

Can I use this for my **portfolio**?   Yes ☐   No ☐
The portfolio is worth 60%.

If yes, tick the appropriate box below.

CORE – submit all 4

* Curriculum Vitae ☐
* Career Investigation ☐
* Summary Report ☐
* Enterprise/Action Plan ☐

OPTIONAL – submit 2 out of 4

* Diary of Work Experience ☐
* Enterprise Report ☐
* Recorded Interview/Presentation ☐
* Report on 'My Own Place' ☐

A total of 6 portfolio items must be submitted.

Now that you've worked through this unit, what are the next steps?

_____
_____
_____

What new **skills** have I acquired?	Did I participate in any **teamwork** activities? If yes, specify.	Useful **Websites** www.irishjobs.ie www.fas.ie Others…

Tasks

* Draft a note on career possibilities.
* State three benefits of a work placement.
* Describe the ways in which participating in the LCVP can improve one's career opportunities.
* Discuss difficulties encountered in your work placement.

CROSS-CURRICULAR

Cross-curricular learning refers to activities or themes which are relevant to many subjects across the curriculum, e.g. health and safety is important in Chemistry, Construction Studies, Engineering, Home Economics and Business.

* What Leaving Certificate subjects were useful? _____

  _____

* How were they useful? _____

  _____

* Were my **V**ocational **S**ubject **G**roupings useful? _____

  _____

MAKING IT HAPPEN...
PREPARING FOR ASSESSMENT

Assessment ideas based on Preparation for the World of Work
Unit 4 – Work Placement

Portfolio of coursework – 60%

Core	Options
★ **Enterprise/Action Plan** - Plan a work placement. ★ **Summary Report** - Report on a work placement, provided you don't submit a Diary of Work Experience in the options.	★ **Diary of Work Experience** ★ **Recorded Interview/Presentation** (a) General interview:1 – 2 questions on your work placement (b) Presentation on work placement, provided you don't submit a Diary of Work Experience

Written Paper – 40%

*Revise the **layout** and **content of your portfolio items**.*

★ Revise the following topics as well:
- Work placement: how to prepare, advantages and disadvantages
- Health and Safety
- Communications
- What you learned from your work placement (skills and knowledge) and how they can be applied to work at home, at school and in the community.

★ Prepare for questions that demonstrate that you participated in a work placement. Don't forget to use the **PEP** approach to structure your answer: **P**re-experience, **E**xperience, **P**ost-experience. Part of the learning cycle of the LCVP is planning, participating and evaluating.

★ Cross-curricular learning – what Leaving Certificate subjects were useful and how? Consider, in particular, your **V**ocational **S**ubject **G**roupings.

★ Analyse your individual contribution and personal performance.

★ Evaluation involves looking at and judging the quality of an activity and asking yourself if you achieved your goals. Consider the following:
- How and why do we evaluate?
- Evaluate your work placement.

Tip: Use your portfolio as a revision tool for the written paper.

SAMPLE EXAM QUESTIONS

These questions are mostly based on this unit only. In the written paper there may be questions which assess a few units together.

Q.1 Work placements (work experience/work shadow) help you to develop an understanding of work and employers' expectations.

(a) Describe the ways in which a work placement (work experience/work shadow) can be evaluated.

(b) Indicate the advantages of a work placement.

(c) Explain the obligations of both employers and employees under the Safety, Health and Welfare Act 1993.

(d) Outline the ways in which a work placement can help you in school, at home and in the community.

Q.2 A work placement is a key component of the LCVP.

(a) Describe ways in which time-keeping may be monitored in the workplace and explain why monitoring is important.

(b) State and explain the steps involved in securing a work placement.

(c) Using appropriate headings, write a brief evaluation of your work placement.

(d) Mention observations you made on health and safety during your work placement.

Q.3 Returning to school after a work placement is not the end of the activity.

(a) Draft a letter of thanks to your employer and explain the benefits to you of the work placement.

(b) Discuss the job-seeking skills which proved beneficial in organising your placement.

(c) State the criteria you would use to assess how successful your placement was.

(d) Why is feedback important?

Q.4 The ability to communicate effectively is an important skill in the workplace.

(a) Why are communications important in the workplace and how can you improve your communication skills?

(b) Explain five personal goals you had in relation to a work placement.

(c) List Leaving Certificate subjects that were useful for your placement and explain how they were useful.

(d) Compare and contrast work experience and work shadowing.

Q.5 A work placement is an opportunity to gain valuable experience in the real world of work.

(a) Describe ways of finding a work placement and discuss the advantages of one of them.

(b) Define teamwork and discuss the benefits of teamwork.

(c) Outline the difficulties you may encounter during a work placement.

(d) List suitable headings for a Diary of a Work Placement.

LINK MODULE 2 – ENTERPRISE EDUCATION

UNIT 1 – ENTERPRISE SKILLS

The purpose of this unit is to introduce you to the skills of enterprise and entrepreneurship such as idea generation, risk assessment, problem solving, teamwork, leadership and commitment. The Specific Learning Outcomes can be achieved through participation in a variety of skill-building exercises and interaction with enterprising adults from the world of business and from the community.

SPECIFIC LEARNING OUTCOMES – SLOs

(as listed in the syllabus)

When you have finished working through this unit, you should be able to:

1.1	describe the qualities and skills of enterprising people
1.2	recognise examples of personal, community and entrepreneurial enterprise
1.3	identify personal strengths and weaknesses
1.4	suggest a course of action appropriate to improving personal enterprise skills
1.5	work co-operatively with others as part of a team
1.6	appreciate the value of teamwork in generating ideas, assessing risks, solving problems and completing tasks
1.7	undertake leadership of a group in an appropriate activity
1.8	plan and organise a meeting
1.9	make a presentation to peers and to adults
1.10	link the activities in this unit to learning in relevant Leaving Certificate subjects
1.11	evaluate the successes achieved and problems encountered in this unit

The aim of the LCVP is to prepare you for further education, seeking employment, and/or planning to start your own business. Enterprise education encourages creativity and problem solving. It helps you to become more open to the idea of setting up your own business in the future. It will also help you to deal with the constantly changing employment situation and our rapidly changing business environment. Enterprise education provides you with an ideal opportunity to be proactive. Enterprising people are assets in all areas within the community whether they are self-employed, an employer or an active citizen.

ENTERPRISE

Enterprise can be defined as the readiness to engage in bold or difficult undertakings. In order to become more enterprising, you must first be aware of the concept of enterprise. Enterprise skills can be observed in local entrepreneurs (people who start their own business). The opportunity to witness at first hand the enterprise skills that they possess can help you to develop an understanding of enterprise in general. Therefore, it's very important to establish links with local businesses and community and voluntary organisations.

We often have a narrow perception of enterprise, associating it with business ventures only! Enterprise affects all aspects of our lives. Enterprise needs to be understood in the broadest possible context:

- Personal Enterprise
- Business Enterprise
- Community Enterprise

Enterprising people are not always entrepreneurs and can be found in all walks of life, e.g. students, employees, voluntary workers etc.

Opportunities to be Enterprising

- School
- Home
- Community
- Personal Life

At School

- You can be enterprising at school by participating in enterprise competitions, e.g. the Student Enterprise Awards or the Celtic Enterprise Programme.
- You can organise fund-raising activities.
- You can set up clubs, e.g. sports clubs or homework clubs.

At Home

- You can be enterprising at home by working from home.
- You can be enterprising by avoiding housework!
- You can rent rooms or run a bed and breakfast.

The Celtic Enterprise Programme teaches young people about enterprise.

In Your Local Community

- You can be enterprising by setting up a youth club.
- You can get involved in local politics.
- You can get involved in charity work.

Contact your Local Enterprise Board.

Remember, entrepreneurial activity in your local community is often on a voluntary basis to help to improve the community.

In Your Personal Life

- ⚙ You can be enterprising by taking courses to develop your talents, e.g. **ECDL**.
- ⚙ You can join a sports club to become fit and healthy.
- ⚙ You can use your skills to help the less fortunate, e.g. doing charity work.

It's important that you appreciate the different ways in which people are enterprising, either personally, in a business, or in the local community.

Record how you think you are enterprising in different areas of your life.

Where am I enterprising?

Enterprising People

Enterprising people are equipped with a certain set of qualities and develop skills and activities to enhance and complement them.

What qualities do I have?

Qualities and Characteristics

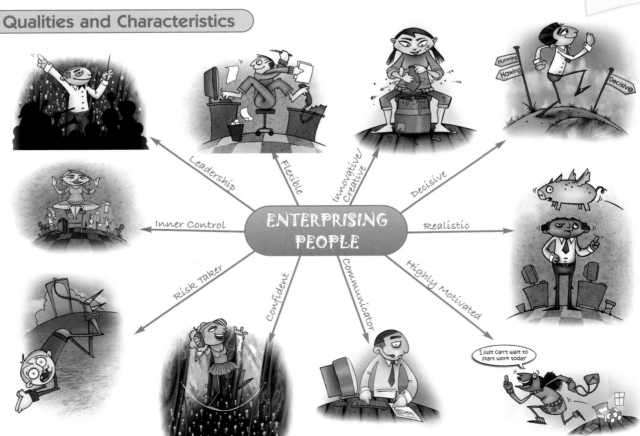

My Personal SWOT Analysis

Another quality that enterprising people usually display is realism. They are realistic about their businesses and about themselves: they know what they are good at and they know what they find challenging or difficult. Part of being realistic is learning to identify your strengths and your weaknesses.

Note: As part of your Enterprise Education you must identify your personal strengths and weaknesses.

My strengths: What's going well for me?

IN SCHOOL	AT HOME	IN THE COMMUNITY

My weaknesses: What's holding me back?

IN SCHOOL	AT HOME	IN THE COMMUNITY

My opportunities: What options are available to me?

IN SCHOOL	AT HOME	IN THE COMMUNITY

My threats: What aspects of my life are to my disadvantage?

IN SCHOOL	AT HOME	IN THE COMMUNITY

It's important to know both your strengths and weaknesses. You can choose to change a **SWOT** analysis to a **SCOT** analysis, where your **Weaknesses** become your **Challenges**. Also it's important to know what **Opportunities** are available to you and to become aware of your **Threats**. **Plan** how to overcome these obstacles.

ENTREPRENEURS

Entrepreneurs are people who have the ability to spot business opportunities, gather the necessary resources, assess risks and take appropriate action to ensure success. They are highly motivated people who calculate risks to achieve their goals. They are essential to our economy. They combine resources such as capital, land and labour to create a successful enterprise. Entrepreneurs need to look before they leap as some businesses will fail. Some people are enterprising within an organisation and this is called **Intrapreneurship**.

Profile of an Entrepreneur

The Global Entrepreneurship Monitor (GEM) 2004 made the following findings about entrepreneurship in Ireland.

WOMEN	MEN
✪ One in every fifty-three women in Ireland has recently set up her own business.	✪ One in every nineteen men in Ireland has recently set up his own business.
✪ Female entrepreneurs are, on average, 38 years old.	✪ Male entrepreneurs are, on average, 34 years old.
✪ Interestingly, women entrepreneurs are more likely to have a higher level of education than their male counterparts.	✪ 42% of men have some third level education, compared to 51% of women.
✪ 42% of women have been working full-time in the home or part-time outside the home prior to setting up their own business.	✪ 79% of men, compared to 58% of women, start their own business having been in full-time employment for several years.

Louise Kennedy is the founder of her own fashion design label.

At the time that the GEM 2004 carried out its research, 193,000 individuals in Ireland were either actively planning to set up their own business or had set up a business within the preceding 42 months. In fact, approximately 2,000 Irish people start new businesses each month.

Part of the reason for this entrepreneurial activity is that the majority of Irish people admire those with the courage to start their own business. Two out of three Irish people think that becoming an entrepreneur is a good career choice, while 85 per cent think that successful entrepreneurs have a very high status.

In the GEM report, one entrepreneur comments on this positive attitude, saying 'People think of entrepreneurs as dynamic, smart and cool! Being an entrepreneur increases a professional's career and personal value and is seen as being a positive innovative trait – whether their entrepreneurial venture is successful or not.'

Profile of a Local Entrepreneur

Prepare a profile of a local entrepreneur using the headings in the box below.
Use these headings to draft a suitable questionnaire.

★ Product/Service	★ They attribute success to …
★ Company	★ Problems – how did they overcome them?
★ Education/Training	
★ Qualities/Characteristics	★ Future Plans

Enterprise – Interview with an Entrepreneur

The following table shows some possible questions to ask during an interview with an entrepreneur.

Name:	Enterprise:
Why did you set up your business?	
What career path did you follow?	
Is training and education important?	
What are your skills and qualities?	
Which skills and qualities are the most important? Why?	
What are the benefits of running your own business?	
What advice would you give to someone starting their own enterprise?	

Feidhlim Byrne with his website www.soccerbot.com

Tip: Interview, write to or e-mail an entrepreneur.

Enterprise – Interview with an Entrepreneur

Plan your interview and make sure you achieve a number of Specific Learning Outcomes.

Is location an important factor?

Does the Single European Market impact on your enterprise?

What financial aid and advice did you receive?

What problems did you encounter?

How do you market your product/service?

How do you ensure targets are reached?

What contribution do you make to your local community?

ACTIVITY

DO I HAVE THE CHARACTERISTICS OF AN ENTREPRENEUR?
Give yourself a score between 1 and 10 depending on how true you think the following statements are of you.
Note: A score of 1 is low and a score of 10 is high. Maximum score is 100.

	CHARACTERISTICS		EXPLANATION	RATINGS SCALE 1-10
1	**Innovative/ Creative**		You come up with new ideas, or find ways of copying or improving on old ones. You show creativity.	
2	**Risk taker**		Entrepreneurs assess and manage risks associated with the venture – both personal and financial risks. You too calculate the possibility of success before any action, i.e. you take measured risks.	
3	**Confident**		You show belief, optimism and assertiveness.	
4	**Decisive**		You are able to make speedy decisions and choose a definite course of action.	
5	**Inner Control**		You are able to take control of your own destiny and are extremely determined.	

	CHARACTERISTICS		EXPLANATION	RATINGS SCALE 1-10
6	Communicator		You are able to communicate well: information is correctly given, received and understood.	
7	Leadership		You get on well with employees and are able to motivate and encourage staff.	
8	Flexible		You are able to alter plans and adapt as situations change.	
9	Realistic		You are able to know what can realistically be achieved and do not strive for the impossible.	
10	Highly Motivated		You need to achieve. You are motivated by money, but also by personal satisfaction. You enjoy working hard.	

Date: _____   My Score [____]

Try this activity again after participating in the **Link Modules.**

Date: _____   My Score [____]

Entrepreneurship in Practice

Idea Generation

Tip: Use idea generation to generate an idea for your enterprise activity.

Every individual has more than ten billion brain cells which have unlimited potential. Most people only use between four and ten per cent of these cells and the rest are just waiting to be used! It's really a myth that only a small percentage of people are creative. Everyone has an **imagination**, which is the fuel for creative thinking. Sometimes we just need to sharpen our saws.

In your LCVP folder have an 'ideas page' to record unusual or interesting ideas. You may decide to use pictures or photographs. Remember ideas are central to any business, so it's important to become innovative and to encourage your own creativity.

Start with the **Paperclip challenge**.

How many uses does a paperclip have?

Try this challenge by yourself.
Next try this challenge in small groups.

Appoint a group leader, a recorder and a motivator. Think of as many uses as possible and aim for quantity rather than quality. Think of wild ideas, no matter how bizarre. Allow ten minutes to record the total number of uses.

Myself   Number of uses   Group   Number of uses

Review the group performance.

Below are some strategies to generate ideas.

* Brainstorming
* Mind maps
* Thinking in new ways
* Finding solutions to problems
* Analysing the failures of others
* Finding new uses for products/services
* Identifying a **niche** market or a gap in the market
* Creating false crises

Idea generation can be used to generate ideas for:

* LCVP activities
* Enterprise activities

From Idea Generation to Generating Sales

Idea Generation

Market Research

SWOT Analysis

Target Market

Competition

Marketing Mix

Test Market

Sales ... Profit

Once you have decided on the product you want to produce or the service you want to provide, you must ensure that it will meet customers' needs. You must have adequate **finance** to buy assets and to cover the day-to-day expenses of the business.

Ownership Options

There are a number of ownership options available to the entrepreneur:
1. A sole-trader is the name given to a business that is owned and run by one person.
2. A partnership describes a business with between two and twenty partners.
3. A company describes one of the following:
    (a) A private limited company
    (b) A public limited company

The big advantage of creating a company is that it has **limited liability**, which means that if the business goes bankrupt, the owners/shareholders will only lose the money they invested. A company can also choose to raise capital through issuing shares.

Your business can also be categorised according to the **number of employees** it has:
1. Small business: 10–50 employees
2. Medium business: 50–250 employees
3. Large business: more than 250 employees

Note: A micro-business has 1–10 employees.

Stakeholders

For a business to succeed it must deal successfully with all of its **stakeholders**. All stakeholders have an interest in the business.

- Employers: The people who hire employees in return for payment. They must abide by all laws governing work and the workplace, e.g. safety, health and welfare regulations. They also have rights and responsibilities.
- Employees: The people who work in return for payment and have certain rights and responsibilities.
- Consumers: The people who buy goods and services. They want quality and after-sales service.
- Suppliers: The people who supply materials.
- Investors: The people who provide finance, e.g. financial institutions. Finance is provided at a cost which is called interest.
- Government: The government decides on laws and taxes.
- Trade Unions: The trade unions represent employees and negotiate for better wages and conditions.
- Local Community: The local community is interested in making sure that environment laws are respected and that infrastructure (shops, schools, roads etc.) is provided. They can affect applications for planning permission by lodging objections.
- Voluntary Organisations: Voluntary organisations may look for sponsorship from local businesses.
- Community Enterprises: Community enterprises encourage local entrepreneurs by offering advice and finance, e.g. County Enterprise Board.
- Family: Entrepreneurs may have to work long hours, which affects family life.
- Competitors: A business has to know its competition because competition can be a threat to a business.

TEAMWORK

A team is a group working together to achieve a common goal/objective. Team building is a **process** and will not happen overnight.

Fill in the following:

BEST TEAM EVER	BEST TEAM EVER
My best personal experience of teamwork was …	What was so special about this team?

Teamwork can enhance the learning in the LCVP classroom and there are many opportunities to experience it during the LCVP.

- ✿ Planning an activity, e.g. a Visit In, a Visit Out is a good exercise in teamwork.
- ✿ Planning and investigating 'My Own Place' provides an opportunity to work as a team.
- ✿ Running an LCVP Enterprise requires that everybody works together.
- ✿ Preparing for assessment, e.g. preparing the Case Study and preparing exam questions with suggested solutions is a perfect chance to practise teamwork.

Advantages of Teams

- ✿ People working together get more work done.
- ✿ Workers take ownership of their work; they have responsibilities to others.
- ✿ Team members share expertise and skills.
- ✿ Working with a team can improve relations, making workers happier.
- ✿ Workers with a common interest can work together.
- ✿ Teamwork encourages participation and communication, thereby avoiding disputes.
- ✿ Teamwork improves interpersonal skills.

An Interesting Team!

Wild Geese

The wild geese fly in a 'V' formation. As each goose flaps its wings it creates a lift for the geese following. Each goose honks to encourage the leader and when the leader gets tired it moves back. When a goose gets sick or wounded, two geese will stay with the goose until it is able to fly or dies and they'll join another 'V' formation.

In the LCVP, four is usually an ideal size for a group/team.
In order to develop team skills there are certain things you must do.

- ✿ You must **listen** to each other.
- ✿ You should **encourage** all team members to participate.
- ✿ You must **record** your findings.
- ✿ You should seek **help** if you need it.

Tip: Try and rotate your role in any team activity, e.g. try being the **leader, the reporter and then the motivator.**

MEETINGS

A meeting is the coming together of at least two people for a lawful purpose.

Planning and Organising a Meeting

The following steps ensure that a meeting is properly organised.
- Send out a notice of the meeting to the people who are invited (usually ten days before it's due to take place).
- Prepare an agenda (a list of items to be discussed).
- Book a room and ensure it's properly prepared (the necessary furniture is there etc.).
- Elect a chairperson and a secretary.
- Adhere to the items on the agenda.
- Only allow one person to speak at a time.
- Allow each item to be properly discussed.
- Make sure a written record is being taken. This record is called the minutes.
- Vote properly where/when needed.
- Decide on any relevant actions to be taken as a result of the meeting.

Important Elements at a Meeting

1. Documents

(a) The Agenda

This is a list of items to be discussed. It should contain the place, date and time of the meeting together with:
- The minutes of the last meeting
- Matters arising from the last meeting
- Correspondence
- Other topics will vary depending on the meeting. (Note: Topics will also vary depending on the organisation, e.g. clubs, business enterprises.)
- A.O.B. (Any Other Business).

(b) The Minutes

These are a brief written record. They contain the following information:
- Who attended the meeting
- The items discussed
- Any decisions made.

2. People

(a) The Chairperson

The Chairperson has many functions. His/her duties include the following:
- He/she convenes the meeting.
- The chairperson ensures that there is a quorum (a minimum number of people present).
- It is the duty of the chairperson to read the minutes, which are then proposed and accepted.
- The chairperson allows people time to speak.
- Putting motions to the vote is the job of the chairperson; he/she also has the casting vote in the event of a tie.
- The chairperson closes the meeting.

(b) The Secretary
- Calls the meeting
- Sends out agendas
- Writes up the minutes.

(c) The Treasurer
- Keeps the accounts
- Lodges all the money
- Pays the bills
- Prepares a financial report for the AGM (Annual General Meeting).

3. Place

Room
- Put a notice on the door.
- Ensure that there are copies of the agenda for everyone.
- Put place cards, pens and paper on the table.
- Check heating, lighting and ventilation.
- Bring flipcharts, an overhead projector or a data projector, if needed.
- Bring an attendance sheet.
- Provide refreshments if a long meeting is expected.

Name a meeting you have attended.

_____

Draft an agenda for a meeting of your choice.

AGENDA

'_____'

The meeting will take place at_____ (time) on _____ (date)
in _____ (place)

1.

2.

3.

4.

5.

6.

Signed: _____   Date: _____
           Secretary

LEARNING BOARD

Briefly summarise the main points using key words from the unit.	Something I **learned**…
	_____
_____	_____
_____	_____
_____	Something I found **difficult**…
_____	_____
_____	_____
_____	_____
_____	Write a short **Case Study** relating to idea generation.
_____	_____
_____	_____
_____	_____
_____	_____

DEVISE AN EXAM QUESTION

Start with a quotation, perhaps a **S**pecific **L**earning **O**utcome or a sentence from this unit.

_____

(a)

(b)

(c)

Write a **6-sentence presentation** on teamwork.

_____

_____

_____

_____

_____

_____

LEARNING BOARD

Can I use this for my **portfolio**?   **Yes** ☐   **No** ☐
The portfolio is worth 60%.

If yes, tick the appropriate box below.

CORE – submit all 4

* Curriculum Vitae ☐
* Career Investigation ☐
* Summary Report ☐
* Enterprise/Action Plan ☐

OPTIONAL – submit 2 out of 4

* Diary of Work Experience ☐
* Enterprise Report ☐
* Recorded Interview/Presentation ☐
* Report on My 'Own Place' ☐

A total of 6 portfolio items must be submitted.

Now that you've worked through this unit, what are the next steps?

_____

_____

What new **skills** have I acquired?	Did I participate in any **teamwork** activities? If yes, specify.	Useful **Websites** www.lcvp.ie www.skool.ie List:
_____ _____ _____	_____ _____	

Tasks

* Write a brief account of leadership.
* List steps to organise a meeting and draft an appropriate agenda for a voluntary organisation.
* Discuss idea generation.

CROSS-CURRICULAR

Cross-curricular learning refers to activities or themes which are relevant to many subjects across the curriculum, e.g. health and safety is important in Chemistry, Construction Studies, Engineering, Home Economics and Business.

* What Leaving Certificate subjects were useful? _____

  _____

* How were they useful? _____

  _____

* Were my **V**ocational **S**ubject **G**roupings useful? _____

  _____

MAKING IT HAPPEN...
PREPARING FOR ASSESSMENT

Assessment ideas based on Enterprise Education
Unit 5 – Enterprise Skills

Portfolio of coursework – 60%

Core

★ **Enterprise/Action Plan**
  - Plan a teamwork activity related to the LCVP.
  - Plan a meeting.
★ **Summary Report**
  - Team activity
  - Improving enterprise skills

Options

★ **Enterprise Report**
  This unit will help you in writing an Enterprise Report but the Enterprise Report is based on a group Enterprise Activity (Unit 4).
★ **Recorded Interview/Presentation**
  (a) General interview: 1–2 questions on teamwork, and enterprise skills.
  (b) Presentation on teamwork.

Written Paper – 40%

Tip: Use your portfolio as a revision tool for the written paper.

*Revise the **layout** and **content of your portfolio items**.*
★ Revise the following topics as well.
  - Skills and qualities of enterprising people
  - Personal, business and community enterprise
  - Teamwork
  - Idea Generation
  - Leadership
  - How to plan and organise a meeting
  - Draft an agenda and minutes of a meeting
  - Chairperson, secretary and treasurer (functions)
  - Profile of an entrepreneur
  - Personal SWOT analysis
  - How to improve personal skills and qualities
★ Prepare for questions regarding an activity you have participated in, e.g. a meeting, a team event, or a visit by an entrepreneur. Don't forget to use the **PEP** approach to structure your answer: **P**re-experience, **E**xperience and **P**ost-experience.
★ Cross-curricular learning – what Leaving Certificate subjects were useful and how? Refer in particular to your **V**ocational **S**ubject **G**roupings.
★ Analyse your individual contribution and personal performance.
★ Evaluation involves looking at and judging the quality of an activity and asking yourself if you achieved your goals. Consider the following:
  - How and why do we evaluate?
  - Evaluate your interview with an entrepreneur.
  - Evaluate group performance.

SAMPLE EXAM QUESTIONS

These questions are mostly based on this unit only. In the written paper there may be questions which assess a few units together.

Q.1 Enterprise skills can be observed in local entrepreneurs.
(a) List five qualities of an enterprising person and state why each quality is important.
(b) Your LCVP class wishes to invite a local entrepreneur to the classroom. Write a letter inviting the entrepreneur. Give him/her a general idea of the kind of structure such a visit might have (e.g. a 10-minute talk followed by 15 minutes of questions) and also highlight any specific areas of interest to the students.
(c) List three personal risks and three business risks associated with entrepreneurship.
(d) Identify skills required for teamwork and explain how each skill is important.

Q.2 Communications skills are essential in an entrepreneur.
(a) Define good communications.
(b) Outline ways of improving your communications skills.
(c) Describe the importance of education and training for entrepreneurship.
(d) List support services available to entrepreneurs and describe some financial incentives available.

Q.3 Enterprising people can be found in a variety of situations.
(a) Identify enterprising people in your local area.
(b) List examples of personal, community and business enterprises.
(c) Discuss leadership and give the characteristics of a successful leader.
(d) Draft a personal SWOT analysis and state the importance of a SWOT analysis.

Q.4 Entrepreneurs are people who have the ability to spot opportunities.
(a) List methods of generating ideas.
(b) Discuss the benefits that entrepreneurs bring to society.
(c) Explain the following words: Agenda, Minutes, Chairperson, Secretary and Treasurer.
(d) List the steps involved in organising a successful meeting.

Q.5 One of the aims of the LCVP is to prepare you to start your own enterprise.
(a) Discuss the importance of planning for an entrepreneur.
(b) Compare the business plan with an Enterprise/Action Plan.
(c) Describe the qualities of an entrepreneur you investigated during the Enterprise Module.
(d) Suggest a course of action appropriate to improving your personal enterprise skills.

LINK MODULE 2 – ENTERPRISE EDUCATION

UNIT 2 – LOCAL BUSINESS ENTERPRISES

The purpose of this unit is to make you aware of what is involved in setting up and running an enterprise. You should be encouraged to meet with entrepreneurs and investigate local business enterprises. Many of the learning outcomes of this unit may be achieved by engaging in a local study of 'My Own Place'. This unit should be integrated with Unit 1 of the Preparation for the World of Work Link Module.

SPECIFIC LEARNING OUTCOMES – SLOs

(as listed in the syllabus)

When you have finished working through this unit, you should be able to:

2.1   identify a range of enterprises in the local community

2.2   understand how an enterprise starts up and what support/training is available

2.3   describe the steps required to plan and carry out an investigation of a local enterprise

2.4   use learning from relevant Leaving Certificate subjects to formulate questions about aspects of a local enterprise

2.5   organise a visit to a local enterprise and invite appropriate speakers to visit the group in school

2.6   carry out a SWOT analysis of a business

2.7   report accurately on a visit by an entrepreneur to the classroom and on a class visit to a local enterprise

2.8   compare and contrast information gathered on a group visit to a local enterprise

2.9   describe a local enterprise with particular reference to products, services, markets and workforce

2.10 understand and describe the different roles of adults working in a business environment

2.11 describe the impact of the Single European Market on a specific enterprise

2.12 describe and evaluate the use of information and communication technologies in a business enterprise

2.13 understand the importance of education and training in the development of a business enterprise

2.14 link the activities in this unit to learning in relevant Leaving Certificate subjects

2.15 evaluate the successes achieved and problems encountered in this unit

LOCAL ENTERPRISES IN YOUR AREA

Enterprises are important to your local area. You should be aware of the number of businesses in your community, the types of businesses and the effect they have. There are many types of enterprises, ranging from your local hairdresser to the local meat-processing plant.

Analyse the main enterprises in your locality below.

Enterprises	Products/Services	Market	No. of Employees

Benefits of Local Enterprises to the Local Area

Enterprises can benefit the area in which they locate. The following are examples of the benefits they can bring:

- They employ local people and have a positive effect on the local economy.
- Other businesses in the area will benefit, e.g. services, banks, transport, etc.
- One business can attract other businesses to the area.
- Enterprises can support local projects, thereby improving the area.
- Enterprises often sponsor local events.
- They may welcome school visits.
- Work placements in local enterprises can provide useful experience.
- Local enterprises may agree to visit the school.
- The product/service may be produced locally, giving prestige to the area.
- Enterprises often help voluntary and community organisations.
- Local infrastructure benefits from the presence of enterprises.

Opportunities for you in a Local Enterprise

Investigating a local enterprise will provide you with an ideal opportunity to learn about businesses and to make contacts for future employment. It will also help you to achieve other Specific Learning Outcomes.

- Work placement (work experience/work shadow)
- Interview for your Career Investigation
- Referees for your Curriculum Vitae
- Employment
- Contacts for the future
- Visit In to the classroom

Evaluating the Success of a Local Enterprise

Success is very important for any business. The following are ways in which success can be measured:

- Profitability and sales: Does the business have high sales and make a profit?
- Continuity of business: How long has the business been in existence?
- Expansion: Has the business grown? Has the number of staff increased?
- Awards: Has the business won any awards?
- Image: How is the business regarded by customers? Does it have a good brand image?
- Low labour turnover: Do employees stay with the business or do they leave after a short time?
- Rising share price: In the case of a company, has the share price risen?

SETTING UP AN ENTERPRISE: RECIPE FOR SUCCESS

There are many difficulties involved in setting up a business: obtaining adequate finance; creating a high quality product/service that will satisfy potential and existing customers; recruiting and retaining the right staff; and choosing the ideal location. You must also try to attract and retain top management, adhere to all legislation and be aware of changes in the economy. To ensure survival, businesses must plan for all of the above. **Good planning is the key to success, whether you are setting up your own enterprise or studying the Link Modules.**

Top 10 Factors in the Success of a Business

Considering the factors below will help a business to ensure that it meets its targets:

1. **Business Plan**: A business plan is necessary to apply for loans and grants. It is also useful as a control mechanism: if you don't plan, you may miss opportunities. Use your business plan to review and evaluate what is happening and to compare planned objectives to actual results.

2. **Finance**
   - ✪ Capital: You need money to start a business (to purchase equipment, machinery, vans etc.).
   - ✪ Grants: Research what tax concessions or grants are available.
   - ✪ Other sources: Finance is also available from a bank overdraft, creditors, or from selling shares.
   - ✪ Cash flow: Cash comes in, cash goes out. This is the money to run the business.

Recipe for success:
Padraig O'Ceidigh has
turned Aer Arann into an
award-winning airline.

3. **Product**: There must be a demand for the product. Market research and the marketing mix are very important in identifying demand.

4. **Staffing**: You must have properly trained staff. Consider the following:
   - ✪ Recruiting procedures
   - ✪ Training
   - ✪ Suitable skills and qualities, e.g. willingness to work overtime when under pressure to meet a deadline
   - ✪ Incentives, e.g. bonus or commission

5. **Location**: The business needs to be in a good location. Pre-existing premises, for example in an industrial park, can be a convenient option. Consider the following:
   - ✪ Transport Services
   - ✪ Employees
   - ✪ Rail/port if exporting
   - ✪ Customers
   - ✪ Suppliers

6. **Managerial Experience**: People setting up and running a business must know what they are doing. To run the business effectively, the following are important:
   - ✪ **Management Skills**: Managers must lead, motivate and communicate.
   - ✪ **Management Activities**: Managers must plan, organise and control.

7. **Laws**: Companies must comply with the law. The following are laws that all businesses must be familiar with:
   - ✪ Health and Safety
   - ✪ Employment Equality
   - ✪ Sale of Goods Act
   - ✪ Young Persons Act
   - ✪ Tax, maternity leave, data protection
   - ✪ Consumer Information Act

8. **Economic Factors**: The economy plays an important role in the success or failure of any business.
   - The Celtic tiger caused low interest rates, low taxation and high employment.
   - Industrial relations: The relationship between management and employees can have a serious effect on a business. Avoiding conflict and resolving issues is very important.
9. **High Quality Product/Service**
10. **Local Environment**: It is essential that businesses obey environment laws.

Business Plan

Business planning is fundamental to the success of a business. A plan is like a road map and will help you to decide whether you should pursue your business idea or try something else.

You are already familiar with the process of planning and with the layout of an **Enterprise/Action Plan**. A business plan is more formal with a lot of detail on all aspects of the business. The business plan is designed to help you work out how you hope to make the business a success.

Elements of a Business Plan

Typically a **business plan** will contain the following:
- Description of business
- Finance
- Production
- Personnel
- Marketing

A BUSINESS PLAN	
DESCRIPTION OF THE BUSINESS	**PERSONNEL**
- The business's legal structure: sole trader, partnership or company - Type of enterprise, e.g. extractive, manufacturing or services - Product/Service	- Expertise, experience - Training - Qualifications and salaries of staff - Management and their responsibilities - Departments and organisation structure
FINANCE	**MARKETING**

- Capital (money required to start a business)
- Loans (money borrowed from financial institutions)
- Accounts:
  - Profit and Loss shows net profit/loss
  - Balance Sheet shows assets and liabilities
  - Cash Flow Forecast shows cash in/cash out
- Sources of finance
	- Market research
	- Target market
	- Marketing mix
	  - Product - Promotion
	  - Price - Place
	(Packaging and personnel are sometimes included in the marketing mix.)
	- Advertising
	- Competition

PRODUCTION	OTHER RELEVANT INFORMATION
✪ Job production: one off, e.g. ship building ✪ Batch production, e.g. a baker ✪ Mass production, e.g. newspapers ✪ Quality ✪ Safety	✪ Leases ✪ Legal documents ✪ CVs ✪ Patents

When constructing a business plan you may need accounting expertise. Ask Accounting and/or Business students to explain any words used above.

Reasons for and Uses of a Business Plan

1. Raising Finance
   - A business plan is a requirement for loans and grants.
   - Planning helps you to decide how much capital you'll need and when it will be needed.

2. Setting Objectives
   - It's a plan for short-term goals, e.g. to maintain a 50 per cent market share.
   - It's a plan for long-term goals, e.g. to expand into a foreign market.

3. Identifying Weaknesses
   - You need to be aware of your weaknesses; they should become your challenges.
   - You can take corrective action if required.

4. Controlling/Evaluating
   - A business plan helps you to monitor progress by allowing you to compare what actually happens with what was planned. You can test achievements and evaluate performance.

5. Timing (Schedule)
   - Both employees and management know what is to be done and when.

6. Decision Making
   - A plan helps management make day-to-day decisions and also helps them to evaluate whether or not it's worthwhile to start or continue the business.

> **Note:** A plan does not have to be a lengthy document.

Comparing the LCVP Enterprise/Action Plan to a Business Plan

ENTERPRISE/ACTION PLAN	BUSINESS PLAN
✪ Objectives ✪ Research Methods ✪ Analysis of Research ✪ Actions ✪ Schedule of Time ✪ Resources and Costs ✪ Evaluation Methods	✪ Business ✪ Product/Service ✪ Personnel ✪ Finance ✪ Marketing ✪ Production ✪ Other Relevant Information

Remember, **both plans** may be assessed in the written paper.

Support and/or Training Available for New Enterprises

When starting a business it's important to be aware of the support and training that is available. The following organisations provide services to new enterprises:

- **City and County Enterprise Boards**: They give advice, training, support and financial assistance to micro-businesses.
- **Údarás na Gaeltachta**: They attract investment to Gaeltacht areas by offering advice, grants and training.
- **FÁS**: They provide training and employment programmes.
- **LEADER Plus programme**: This programme promotes development in rural areas.
- **Small Firms' Association**: They provide support and advice to small firms.
- **Financial Institutions**: They provide advice and finance.
- **Enterprise Ireland**: They provide support and grants to Irish firms.
- **Fáilte Ireland:** This is a semi-state body that promotes tourism.
- **Bord Iascaigh Mhara**: This is a state agency that promotes the fishing industry.

Grants

The following are examples of grants available from City and County Enterprise Boards:

- **Capital Grants** – a maximum of 50% of the cost of fixed assets, not exceeding a €75,000 grant
- **Employment Grant** – a maximum of €7,500 per job, subject to a limit of 10 jobs and a total grant sum of €75,000
- **Feasibility Study Grants** – a maximum of 50% of the cost of a feasibility study, subject to a limit of €5,100

LOCAL ENTERPRISE INVESTIGATION

The Local Enterprise Investigation provides you with an ideal opportunity to participate in teamwork. It is also an ideal opportunity to develop links between your school and companies.

Planning your Local Enterprise Investigation

Good planning is the key to success, whether setting up an enterprise, studying the Link Modules, or preparing to do a Local Enterprise Investigation. Bear the following points in mind when you are preparing to start your investigation:

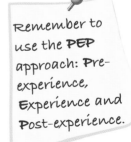

Remember to use the **PEP** approach: Pre-experience, Experience and Post-experience.

- Use the LCVP Enterprise/Action Plan template.
- Get as much information as you can about the enterprise before you start the investigation proper. Has the company got a website?
- You need to be very clear from the start about exactly what information you need to get to complete your investigation. Consider the **SLOs**.
- Consider time constraints. Can you get everything done on time?
- Be aware of the assessment criteria, both for the written paper and for the portfolio. Ask yourself, 'Can I incorporate this investigation into my portfolio?'
- Ensure that this activity is relevant to the LCVP and make sure that you achieve the **S**pecific **L**earning **O**utcomes (SLOs).
- Plan a Visit In/Visit Out.

Important Aspects of Local Enterprise

While conducting your local enterprise investigation, there are certain aspects that you should make sure you pay close attention to. You will need to address these in your investigation.

- **Information and Communications Technology (ICT)**
- **Personnel: The Role of Adults in the Workplace**
- **Single European Market**
- **SWOT Analysis**
- **Education and Training**

Information and Communications Technology

ICT has many uses for enterprises. Find out which of the following technologies your chosen local enterprise uses. Ask them how important they are to the enterprise.

1. **The Internet**: The Internet is a fantastic method of researching information. Businesses can also develop their own websites and market products/services worldwide, e.g. www.folens.ie.
2. **E-mail**: This is a cheap way of communicating worldwide.
3. **Mobile phones**: Mobile phones allow us to contact people while they are travelling (in a taxi, on the street etc.) or when they are in an otherwise remote location.
4. **Portable computers**: Lap-tops give people the freedom to 'connect' to their office even when they are away from it, allowing them to work while on a train or from home, for example.
5. **Video-conferencing**: Video-conferencing links people by using computer and TV screens and is ideal for holding meetings with people all over the world, saving time and money that would otherwise be spent travelling abroad to meetings.
6. **Electronic data interchange**: This allows one computer to connect to another. Stock orders, invoices etc. can be sent from one computer to another with greater speed.

Businesses also have many uses for computers packages:
- **Word-processing** is used to type letters and reports.
- **Spreadsheets** are used for accounts and the payroll.
- **Databases** are used to file employee and customer records.

The following are some advantages and disadvantages of using ICT:

ADVANTAGES	DISADVANTAGES
• Technology eliminates boundaries worldwide. • It's possible to work from home. • Advertising is cheaper on the Internet. • Sending messages is cheap using e-mail, for example. • Mass production has made technology more affordable.	• You have to invest a lot of money in technology at first, i.e. capital expenditure. • Staff have to be trained to use the technology. • Intellectual property rights: copyright programs are expensive. • Technology must be constantly up-dated. • Fraud can be a problem.

The ability to use ICT's such as computers and audio-visual equipment is a skill relevant in school, further education, when seeking employment or planning to start your own business. The LCVP will provide you with many opportunities to develop ICT skills. In the LCVP, you should be able to do the following:

 ✿ Enter, edit, store, retrieve and print information.
 ✿ Word-process CVs, letters and reports and create illustrated documents.
 ✿ Access and use relevant information from CD-ROMs and from the Internet.
 ✿ Send and receive e-mail messages.

Single European Market

The Single European Market is a group of 25 countries who promote free movement of goods, services, capital and labour among member countries. Some members also have a common currency – the euro. This has simplified trade and travel in the eurozone.

Impact of the Single European Market

1. Irish companies have access to wider European markets.
2. Irish companies face more competition. As a result, they have to become more competitive and unfortunately some may close, which may lead to redundancies.
3. Many international companies are locating in Ireland to gain access to the European market.
4. Currency: the introduction of the euro has made it easier to do business in the eurozone. The eurozone is made up of those countries within the EU who have the euro as their currency. Trading outside of the eurozone will leave companies exposed to the risk of currency fluctuations.
5. Irish companies have to compete with low-wage eastern European countries.
6. Documentation when trading with EU countries is easier.
7. Recognition of qualifications within the EU provides more job opportunities.
8. Financial institutions are able to open branches in any member state.
9. Sales can be increased, which can lead to economies of scale – the more products a company produces, the lower the cost of the product.
10. All contracts over €50,000 for the supply of goods and services to EU governments must be tendered to all EU members. This is known as Public Procurement.
11. There are extra costs involved in the following:
    • Packaging, transport etc.
    • Interpreters and translators: foreign language skills are needed to trade with other countries. A foreign language is also a requirement of the LCVP.
    • Advertising abroad
    • Adapting products to EU standards and legislation.

The European Union

The EU presently has 25 countries forming a market of nearly 500 million people. Other countries are currently negotiating their entry into the European Union. The 25 member states of the European Union are:
Austria, Belgium, Cyprus, Czech Republic, Denmark, Estonia, Finland, France, Germany, Greece, Hungary, Ireland, Italy, Latvia, Lithuania, Luxembourg, Malta, Netherlands, Poland, Portugal, Slovakia, Slovenia, Spain, Sweden, and the United Kingdom.

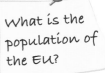

What is the population of the EU?

Importance of Education and Training

A wide range of training, education and expertise is required when starting an enterprise and this is an issue that you should address in your local enterprise investigation. Interestingly, individuals who are more educated are more likely to pursue entrepreneurship. The GEM 2004 published in their report that 71 per cent of women entrepreneurs and 54 per cent of male entrepreneurs have some third level or post-graduate education. It is important to acknowledge, however, that many entrepreneurs (particularly male) have not completed any third level education before starting their own businesses. It is likely, though, that many of these will do training courses, while running their enterprises, in order to ensure that their skills are up to date. Confidence and role models also have a positive effect on entrepreneurship. Research shows that people whose teachers often talked about entrepreneurship have a greater belief in their own ability to set up a business, with the result that they are more likely to do just that. Be sure to find out about the levels of training, education and expertise in the enterprise you are investigating.

SWOT Analysis

A SWOT analysis is an ideal way to assess and investigate a local business. You should be able to identify the strengths and weaknesses (challenges) which are part of the business's current situation and also identify the opportunities and threats that it will encounter in the future.

Strengths: These are the strong points in the current situation, e.g. product/service, trademark, brand name (Levi's), location, assets etc.

Weaknesses: These are areas that need to be developed, e.g. the product/service may need to be updated or employees may not have the necessary skills.

Opportunities: These are part of the future possibilities and potential of the business, e.g. new products, new markets, more employees.

Threats: These are the potential dangers, e.g. competition, loss of market share, loss of customers, changes in legislation, changes in the economy.

Sometimes a SWOT analysis may be referred to as a SCOT analysis: Strengths, Challenges, Opportunities and Threats.

> A SWOT analysis can be used to examine all LCVP activities.

Strengths	Weaknesses/Challenges
✿ Advantages ✿ What is done well	✿ Disadvantages ✿ What is done badly
Opportunities	**Threats**
✿ Markets ✿ New Trends ✿ Events	✿ Competition ✿ Changes in technology ✿ Changes in legislation or government policy ✿ Changes in tastes

Sample SWOT Analysis of an Enterprise

SinCom

This analysis will be done on a web design company set up by an enterprising student. The name of the company is SinCom.

My **SWOT** becomes my **SCOT** as my weaknesses become my challenges.

STRENGTHS

- ⚙ I am a hard-working, determined and creative person with excellent IT skills.
- ⚙ I am an unusual person as I have both the necessary skills to manage my business successfully and the necessary skills to provide my service.
- ⚙ I also have access to professional backup.

WEAKNESSES/CHALLENGES

- ⚙ Time constraints: I am an LCVP student studying for my Leaving Certificate. This is an issue I have to tackle using time management.
- ⚙ Age constraints: I am too young to drive. This limits the range of potential customers I can reach.

OPPORTUNITIES

- ⚙ The Internet is the fastest growing form of media ever known to man. The market for SinCom's IT services is enormous and growing.
- ⚙ Setting up my own enterprise gives me the opportunity to learn all the necessary skills for running my own business in the future – 'Enterprise is for life.'
- ⚙ In Ireland, IT businesses are not exploited to the fullest. This is an opportunity for SinCom to promote the importance of its IT services to the business world.

THREATS

- ⚙ Established e-commerce companies with specialist people to look after finance, production, sales, etc. are a threat.
- ⚙ Other enterprises in the school provide competition.
- ⚙ Changes in technology mean that the business has to keep changing and developing.

ACTIVITY

Prepare a **SWOT** analysis on a business of your choice.

Challenges Facing Businesses

Businesses face many **uncertainties** and must be able to **overcome** these challenges.

Possible uncertainties facing a business	How to overcome these challenges
1. Sales level and demand may change	☼ Advertise on an ongoing basis. ☼ Conduct market research constantly. ☼ Maintain competitive prices. ☼ Introduce new products. ☼ Keep up with changing tastes and laws.
2. Difficulties recruiting skilled staff	☼ Pay competitive wages. ☼ Train staff. ☼ Have official perks, e.g. a company car. ☼ Establish links with a college. ☼ Pay college fees for employees who wish to study.
3. Availability of adequate raw materials	☼ Produce your own raw materials. ☼ Have several suppliers. ☼ Develop and source new types of raw materials.
4. Profitability	☼ Control costs. ☼ Ensure an adequate mark-up. ☼ Ensure quality.
5. Competition	☼ Maintain excellent customer service. ☼ Build up customer loyalty.
6. Foreign markets	☼ Take advantage of the enlargement of the EU. Research new member states as potential customers. Research their tastes and laws. ☼ Standardise products/services to meet the needs of foreign markets. ☼ Trade with countries using the euro.

Personnel: The Role of Adults in the Workplace

All stakeholders, who are usually adults, play a role in the workplace. They include the owners (shareholders), the manager (the leader), the secretary, employees (skilled, semi-skilled and unskilled), the Health and Safety Officer and the Shop Steward (the union representative).

Tool for Carrying Out Local Enterprise Investigation: Questionnaire

A questionnaire is an ideal way of obtaining information about a company. The success of a questionnaire really depends on asking the right questions.

Consider the following when drafting a questionnaire:
1. What do you want to find out about the enterprise? What information do you need?
2. Brainstorm a list of possible headings that you could group the required information under. Use the Specific Learning Outcomes.
3. Make up questions for each of the headings you have selected.
4. Work in teams.

10 Key Headings for Possible Questions

HEADINGS	POSSIBLE QUESTIONS
1. Company/Product/Service	
2. Personnel	
3. Marketing	
4. Legislation	
5. Information and Communications Technology	
6. Industrial Relations	
7. Finance	
8. Production	
9. Support	
10. Single European Market	

LOCAL ENTERPRISE INVESTIGATION – QUESTIONNAIRE

The following table shows some possible questions to include in a questionnaire for a local business enterprise.

Tip: You may decide to design your own questionnaire.

VISIT OUT	Name: Date: Time: Details of Visit:		Duration:

Company
Name: Website:

Type of Organisation

Sole trader ☐   Partnership ☐   Private company ☐   Public Company ☐

Other ☐

Classification

Extractive ☐   Construction ☐   Manufacturing ☐   Tertiary ☐

Comment _____

_____

History of Company

_____

Products/Services

_____

Personnel
Management _____
Skills relevant _____   Activities relevant _____
Qualities of management _____

Employees
No. of employees _____

Male ☐   Female ☐

   - Who recruits? _____
   - How do you recruit? _____
   - What type of training do you offer? _____
   - What skills and qualities do you look for? _____
   - Do you encounter any issues with diversity? _____
   - What's the dress code? _____
Are you willing to participate in a work placement for students? Yes ☐ No ☐

Marketing

What type of market research do you engage in?

Desk ☐   Field ☐

- Who's your target market? _____

- What percentage of the market share does your company have? _____

- Who's your competition? _____

- Discuss your marketing mix.

    - Product _____

    - Price_____

    - Place _____

    - Promotion _____

- How do you get publicity? _____

- Which forms of promotion does your company use? _____

Personal Selling ☐   Advertising ☐

Public Relations ☐   Sales Promotion ☐

Legislation

- Has the company got a Health & Safety Statement? _____

- How do you train personnel with regard to health and safety? _____

- List the main reasons for accidents in the workplace. _____

_____

- What's the minimum wage you pay? _____

- Do you promote equality and how? _____

ICT

Do you use ICT? List examples._____

_____

Does ICT play a major role? How? _____

_____

Have technological changes helped or hindered your business?_____

_____

_____

Industrial Relations

Are employees members of trade unions? Name the trade unions._____

_____

Give typical examples of conflict. _____

_____

How does the company deal with conflicts?_____

_____

Finance

Has the company borrowed?   Yes ☐   No ☐

Name the financial institution/s it has borrowed from._____

_____

Did the company receive grants? Comment. _____

List other sources of finance._____

_____

Production

List type: Job ☐   Batch ☐   Mass ☐   Other ☐

Where do you source your raw materials?_____

How do you ensure quality? _____

_____

Support

List any agencies that have assisted your company._____

_____

CEB (City and County Enterprise Board) ☐   Other ☐

What type of support did you receive?_____

_____

Europe

What impact has the Single European Market had on your business?_____

_____

Is it important to have knowledge of a foreign language? _____

_____

Does location matter? Elaborate._____

_____

Evaluation of Local Enterprise Investigation

After you have completed your investigation, don't forget to **evaluate**:

* **The investigation**
  - Have all areas been covered for assessment purposes?
* **The team**
  - Did the group work well?
  - Did anyone dominate the group?
  - Did everyone contribute?
  - Were there any challenges?
  - How did the group come to a consensus and solve problems?

LEARNING BOARD

Briefly summarise the main points using key words from the unit.	Something I **learned**…
	Something I found **difficult**…
	Write a short **Case Study** relating to a local enterprise.

DEVISE AN EXAM QUESTION

Start with a quotation, perhaps a **S**pecific **L**earning **O**utcome or a sentence from this unit.

(a)

(b)

(c)

Write a **6-sentence presentation** on a SWOT analysis.

LEARNING BOARD

Can I use this for my **portfolio**?　　**Yes** ☐　　**No** ☐
The portfolio is worth 60%.

If yes, tick the appropriate box below.

CORE – submit all 4

* Curriculum Vitae ☐
* Career Investigation ☐
* Summary Report ☐
* Enterprise/Action Plan ☐

OPTIONAL – submit 2 out of 4

* Diary of Work Experience ☐
* Enterprise Report ☐
* Recorded Interview/Presentation ☐
* Report on 'My Own Place' ☐

A total of 6 portfolio items must be submitted.

Now that you've worked through this unit, what are the next steps?

_____

_____

What new **skills** have I acquired?	Did I participicate in any **teamwork** activities? If yes, specify.	Useful **Websites** www.lcvp.ie List:

Tasks

* Identify the impact of the Single European Market.
* State three benefits of ICT.
* Are education and training relevant to entrepreneurship?

CROSS-CURRICULAR

Cross-curricular learning refers to activities or themes which are relevant to many subjects across the curriculum, e.g. health and safety is important in Chemistry, Construction Studies, Engineering, Home Economics and Business.

* What Leaving Certificate subjects were useful? _____

_____

* How were they useful? _____

_____

* Were my **V**ocational **S**ubject **G**roupings useful? _____

_____

MAKING IT HAPPEN...
PREPARING FOR ASSESSMENT

Assessment ideas based on Enterprise Education
Unit 6 – Local Business Enterprises

Portfolio of coursework – 60%

Core

★ **Enterprise/Action Plan**
 - Plan an investigation of local enterprises.
 - Plan a visit to a local enterprise.
 - Plan a visit to the classroom by an entrepreneur.

★ **Summary Report**
 - Local enterprises
 - A Visit In to the classroom
 - A Visit Out to an enterprise

Options

★ **Enterprise Report**
 This unit will help you in writing an Enterprise Report but remember the Enterprise Report is based on a group Enterprise Activity (Unit 4).

★ **Recorded Interview/Presentation**
 (a) General interview: 1–2 questions on this unit.
 (b) Presentation on teamwork and local enterprises, for example.

Written Paper – 40%

Tip: Use your portfolio as a revision tool for the written paper.

*Revise the **layout** and **content of your portfolio items**.*

★ Revise the following topics as well.
 - Discuss local enterprises and the elements of a successful enterprise.
 - How to prepare for a Visit In.
 - How to prepare for a Visit Out.
 - SWOT analysis
 - Success of an enterprise, how to ensure targets are met, how an enterprise can benefit a locality, how to overcome challenges
 - Impact of the Single European Market
 - Use of ICT
 - Business plans: layout and reasons for writing a plan
 - The importance of education and training

★ Prepare for questions regarding an activity you have participated in, e.g. an investigation of local enterprises, a visit to an enterprise, a visit by an entrepreneur. Don't forget to use the **PEP** approach to structure your answer: **P**re-experience, **E**xperience and **P**ost-experience. Part of the learning cycle of the LCVP is planning, participating and evaluating.

★ Cross curricular learning – what Leaving Certificate subjects were useful and how? Consider, in particular, your **V**ocational **S**ubject **G**roupings.

★ Analyse your individual contribution and personal performance.

★ Evaluation involves looking at and judging the quality of an activity and asking yourself if you achieved your goals. Consider the following:
 - How and why do we evaluate?
 - Evaluate an activity.
 - Evaluate group performance/teamwork.

SAMPLE EXAM QUESTIONS

These questions are mostly based on this unit only. In the written paper there may be questions which assess a few units together.

Q.1 A Visit Out activity can be an extremely interesting experience and a great LCVP learning opportunity.

(a) Describe the steps involved in preparing for the visit and explain why your class undertook this visit.

(b) List appropriate headings for an Enterprise Action/Plan.

(c) Write a letter to a friend in America describing what you have learned from the visit.

(d) Identify four methods that you could use to evaluate this visit and discuss the advantages of each method.

Q.2 As part of the Link Modules you are encouraged to meet with entrepreneurs and investigate local business enterprises.

(a) Describe an enterprise you investigated.

(b) Apply a SWOT analysis to the above enterprise.

(c) Describe the roles of different adults working in this enterprise.

(d) Comment on why this enterprise has been successful and highlight any challenges facing this enterprise.

Q.3 You have been asked to investigate a local enterprise and finally to draft a report.

(a) List headings/sections that would appear in the report.

(b) Who would benefit from this report and why?

(c) Coping with uncertainties is a challenge for most enterprises. Outline the uncertainties that enterprises face and suggest how they can plan for these uncertainties.

(d) Discuss the importance of education and training and the impact of the Single European market.

Q.4 You must organise a meeting to prepare for a Visit Out.

(a) What steps should you take to organise the meeting?

(b) Draft an agenda for the meeting and describe how to evaluate the meeting.

(c) List the objectives of a Visit Out and identify the steps you need to take to plan for a Visit Out.

(d) Describe the different ways in which an enterprise can benefit a local community.

LINK MODULE 2 – ENTERPRISE EDUCATION

UNIT 3 – LOCAL VOLUNTARY ORGANISATIONS / COMMUNITY ENTERPRISES

This unit introduces you to enterprises other than commercial businesses. You are encouraged to find out how these enterprises are organised, how they are funded and how they contribute to local development. The outcomes of this unit can be achieved by a combination of classroom teaching, analysis of Case Studies, out-of-school investigations and invited visitors to the classroom. As part of this unit, it is recommended that you engage in a local study of 'My Own Place'. This unit should be integrated with Unit 1 of the Preparation for the World of Work Link Module.

SPECIFIC LEARNING OUTCOMES – SLOs

(as listed in the syllabus)

When you have finished working through this unit, you should be able to:

3.1	describe the qualities and skills of enterprising people
3.1	identify the voluntary bodies that carry out community work in the locality
3.2	describe the work carried out by a range of voluntary groups in the locality
3.3	understand and describe the different roles of adults working in voluntary community organisations
3.4	organise a visit to a local community enterprise and/or invite an appropriate speaker to visit the group in school
3.5	use learning from relevant Leaving Certificate subjects to formulate questions about aspects of community enterprise
3.6	integrate information from a variety of sources to prepare a report, plan or presentation on an aspect of community development
3.7	link the activities in this unit to learning in relevant Leaving Certificate subjects
3.8	evaluate the successes achieved and problems encountered in this unit

As an LCVP student you should be aware of the range of voluntary and community activities in your area and the contribution that such activities make to community development.

You may decide to **profile** these community enterprises and voluntary organisations and/or invite **a speaker** from the organisation to the classroom. A possible **follow–on activity** may be **a fund-raiser** for this organisation. If you decide to do this as your LCVP Enterprise Activity, remember to use the **PEP** approach: **P**re-experience, **E**xperience and **P**ost-experience.

Ensure you know at least one community and one voluntary organisation **in detail**. Having a **general overview** of a number of community and voluntary organisations is also essential as these may be assessed in the written paper.

VOLUNTARY ORGANISATIONS

A **voluntary organisation** can be defined as a group of people who have come together on a voluntary basis with the expressed aim of improving the lives of others in the community. These can be divided into local and national organisations.

Local Voluntary Groups/Organisations	National Voluntary Organisations	
Tidy Towns Committee Youth Club Drama Club Homework Club Neighbourhood Watch	Society of St Vincent de Paul The Alzheimer Society of Ireland Amnesty International The Rehab Group Trocáire The GAA Order of Malta Focus Ireland Macra na Feirme	Gorta Aware Bóthar Irish Red Cross An Óige

These national voluntary organisations may have local branches.

What do Voluntary Organisations Actually do?

Voluntary organisations play an increasingly significant role in all areas of life. Some are localised and deal with a range of diverse issues: some promote the development of the local community, e.g. Tidy Towns Committees; others provide protection, e.g. Neighbourhood Watch. A number of voluntary organisations focus on disadvantaged groups within society, e.g. Society of St Vincent de Paul. They can also be involved in sports, e.g. the GAA. Many voluntary groups also promote drama and music.

The Gaelic Athletic Association – GAA	St Vincent de Paul
The GAA was established to revive and nurture traditional indigenous pastimes, through the presentation and promotion of hurling, Gaelic football, handball, Irish dancing, music and song. There are over 2,500 clubs in Ireland alone.	This is a voluntary organisation whose membership is open to people of all faiths. It aims to help people in need on an individual basis, by providing clothing, fuel, food, beds, furniture and holidays.

Focus Ireland	Macra Na Feirme
Focus Ireland believes that everyone has a right to a place that they can call home. They try to empower homeless people (give them the power to help themselves) by providing information, resources and training, enabling them to rejoin society.	Macra na Feirme aims to promote agriculture and rural development. It organises activities around eight different programme areas: sports and social, travel, competitions, art and culture, farming, rural development, education and leadership training.

Benefits of Voluntary Organisations

- ☼ They provide a service not otherwise available.
- ☼ They help the less well off in society, so everybody has at least a basic standard of living, e.g. the elderly, the underprivileged.
- ☼ They provide a good example to young people and may encourage them to get involved and improve their skills.
- ☼ They foster greater community spirit, which leads to more support when community projects are undertaken.
- ☼ Individuals involved benefit enormously as they are more committed to their local community.

Invite a speaker from a voluntary organisation to the LCVP class.

Evaluation in Voluntary Organisations

Evaluation is also important for voluntary organisations. **Why?** To evaluate means to look at and judge the quality or value of something. It is important for organisations to take a close look at themselves and what they are doing on a regular basis.

- ☼ Evaluation is important because it allows the organisation to review what it has achieved.
- ☼ The organisation's achievements can be compared to its objectives.
- ☼ Evaluation provides an opportunity to plan ahead, make improvements and branch out into new areas.
- ☼ It is a chance to check that funds are being properly used.

Local voluntary organisations face problems, e.g. lack of finance, volunteers and skills.

People Involved in Voluntary Organisations

Most people involved in voluntary organisations work on a voluntary basis. Some people are paid and work on a full-time or part-time basis. People involved in these organisations have different roles, e.g. counsellors, fund-raisers, coaches, managers and administrators to name a few.

COMMUNITY ENTERPRISES

A **community enterprise** can be defined as a small commercial enterprise that has been established for the benefit of the local community rather than an individual.
The following are examples of community enterprises:

☼ FÁS	☼ LEADER Plus Programme
☼ City/County Enterprise Boards	☼ County Development Boards
☼ Údarás na Gaeltachta	☼ Teagasc

What do Community Enterprises Actually do?

Community enterprises promote development in particular communities: Údarás na Gaeltachta works in Gaeltacht areas; LEADER Plus programmes promote rural enterprises; and City and County Enterprise Boards promote the development of micro-businesses with between one and ten employees.

FÁS	City & County Enterprise Boards
FÁS operates training and employment programmes and recruitment services. It also provides support for businesses, cooperatives and community-based enterprises.	These provide support services to small businesses throughout the country. They provide advice and training grants. They also promote entrepreneurship through the Enterprise Awards Scheme and Enterprise Encounter.
Údarás na Gaeltachta	**LEADER Plus Programmes**
Its aim is to preserve and strengthen the Gaeltacht and the Irish language so that strong, self-confident communities can emerge, achieve their full potential and enjoy a high quality of life. This can be achieved by attracting investment to the Gaeltacht regions and offering grants and incentives.	This is an EU initiative for rural development. It enables groups in rural areas to implement their own business plans for the development of their areas. It is co-funded by the Irish Government and the EU.

Benefits of Community Enterprises

- Community enterprises help to reduce unemployment.
- They generate income and provide services.
- They restore community pride.
- They improve the local environment.
- They help those who are socially excluded.
- They provide a service not otherwise available.
- They foster greater community spirit which leads to more support when community projects are undertaken.
- Sometimes they receive grants which are utilised locally.

Contrast Voluntary Organisations and Business Enterprises

There are **differences** between voluntary organisations and enterprises.

Voluntary Organisations	Commercial/Business Enterprises
They are non-profit making.	They trade for a profit.
Volunteers **may** receive payment.	Staff receive payment.
Finance comes from grants, fund-raising, the Lotto.	Finance comes from investors and they charge for products/services.
They may not have a risk element.	They have a risk element.

ACTIVITY

VOLUNTARY ORGANISATIONS AND COMMUNITY ENTERPRISES – WEBLINKS

Using the following websites, divide into **groups** and access information. Complete a profile using the templates on p. 185 and p. 186. Draft a report on your findings. File in your **LCVP folder**.

www.fas.ie	FÁS
www.udaras.ie	Údarás na Gaeltachta
www.comhairle.ie	National Information Agency for the Public Services
www.cdb.ie	County Development Boards
www.adm.ie	Contact details for Partnerships and Community Groups
www.rehab.ie	Training Centres and Enterprises that promote Equality
www.fairtrade.ie	Irish Fairtrade Organisation
www.goal.ie	GOAL – Relief Organisation
www.trocaire.ie	Trócaire – Relief Organisation
www.focusireland.ie	Supporting Homeless People
www.antaisce.org	National Trust for Ireland
www.inou.ie	Irish National Organisation for the Unemployed
www.oasis.gov.ie	Oasis is an Irish e-Government system providing access to comprehensive information on public services.
www.environ.ie/localindex.html	Find your Local Authority website here

Profile of a Voluntary Organisation: Possible Template for Rough Work

Using the following template, profile an organisation of your choice, e.g. **Trócaire**.

TRÓCAIRE

PROFILE OF A VOLUNTARY ORGANISATION	
Name of organisation:	
What services does the organisation provide?	
Who benefits from the organisation?	Website: **Contact Details** Phone: Fax: E-mail:
How is the organisation financed? Does it raise funds from voluntary contributions? How?	Is it run by volunteers and/or staff? What are their roles?
How successful is the organisation?	
What does the day-to-day running of the organisation involve?	
What is the organisation's role in the community?	

Tip: Ensure you know at least one voluntary organisation in **detail** for the written exam.

To source information on voluntary organisations, look up websites, write a letter, e-mail a local representative or invite a speaker from the organisation to give a talk. A follow-on activity may be to do a fund-raiser for this organisation.

Profile of a Community Enterprise: Possible Template for Rough Work

Using the following template, profile a community enterprise of your choice, e.g. FÁS.

PROFILE OF A COMMUNITY ENTERPRISE	
Name of organisation:	
What services does the enterprise provide?	
Who benefits from the enterprise?	Website: **Contact Details** Phone: Fax: E-mail:
How is the enterprise financed? Does it raise funds from voluntary contributions? How?	Is it run by volunteers and/or staff? What are their roles?
How successful is the enterprise?	
What does the day-to-day running of the enterprise involve?	
What is the enterprise's role in the community?	

*Tip: Ensure you know at least one community enterprise in **detail** for the written exam.*

To source information on community enterprises, look up their websites, write a letter, e-mail a local representative and/or invite a speaker from the community enterprise to give a talk.

LEARNING BOARD

Briefly summarise the main points using key words from the unit.	Something I **learned**...
	_____
	_____
	_____
	Something I found difficult...
	_____
	_____
	_____
	Write a short **Case Study** relating to a community enterprise.
	_____
	_____
	_____

DEVISE AN EXAM QUESTION

Start with a quotation, perhaps a **S**pecific **L**earning **O**utcome or a sentence from this unit.

_____

(a)

(b)

(c)

Write a **6-sentence presentation** on a voluntary organisation.

_____

_____

_____

_____

_____

LEARNING BOARD

Can I use this for my **portfolio**?   Yes ☐   No ☐
The portfolio is worth 60%.

If yes, tick the appropriate box below.

CORE – submit all 4

* Curriculum Vitae ☐
* Career Investigation ☐
* Summary Report ☐
* Enterprise/Action Plan ☐

OPTIONAL – submit 2 out of 4

* Diary of Work Experience ☐
* Enterprise Report ☐
* Recorded Interview/Presentation ☐
* Report on 'My Own Place' ☐

A total of 6 portfolio items must be submitted.

Now that you've worked through this unit, what are the next steps?

_____
_____

What new **skills** have I acquired?	Did I participate in any **teamwork** activities? If yes, specify.	Useful **Websites**
_____ _____ _____	_____ _____ _____	www.svp.ie www.gorta.ie www.trocaire.ie Others…

Tasks

* Write an account of a visitor from a voluntary organisation.
* List ideas on how to source information on voluntary organisations/community enterprises.
* How does the work of voluntary organisations contribute to local developments in the community?
* Describe how you would organise a visitor from a community enterprise.

CROSS-CURRICULAR

Cross-curricular learning refers to activities or themes which are relevant to many subjects across the curriculum, e.g. health and safety is important in Chemistry, Construction Studies, Engineering, Home Economics and Business.

* What Leaving Certificate subjects were useful? _____

_____

* How were they useful? _____

_____

* Were my **V**ocational **S**ubject **G**roupings useful? _____

_____

MAKING IT HAPPEN...
PREPARING FOR ASSESSMENT

Assessment ideas based on Enterprise Education
Unit 7 – Local Voluntary Organisations/Community Enterprises

Portfolio of coursework – 60%

Core

★ **Enterprise/Action Plan**
  - Plan an investigation into a voluntary organisation/community enterprise.
  - Plan a visit to/from a voluntary organisation/community enterprise.
★ **Summary Report**
  - Investigate a voluntary organisation.
  - Visit or organise a visit from a voluntary organisation/community enterprise.

Options

★ **'My Own Place' Report**
★ **Recorded Interview/Presentation**
  (a) General interview: 1–2 questions on this unit.
  (b) Presentation on a Visit In, Visit Out, community enterprise or voluntary organisation.

Tip: Use your portfolio as a revision tool for the written paper.

Written Paper – 40%

*Revise the **layout** and **content of your portfolio items**.*
★ Revise the following topics as well.
  - Be aware of at least one voluntary organisation and one community enterprise in detail and have a general overview of a number of voluntary organisations and a number of community enterprises.
  - Be aware of how voluntary organisations and community enterprises benefit a local community.
  - Compare voluntary organisations with business organisations.
★ Prepare for questions that demonstrate that you have participated in an activity, e.g. a Visit In, Visit Out or an investigation of voluntary organisations/community enterprises. Don't forget to use the **PEP** approach to structure your answer: **P**re-experience, **E**xperience, **P**ost-experience. Part of the learning cycle of the LCVP is planning, participating and evaluating.
★ Cross-curricular learning – what Leaving Certificate subjects were useful and how? Discuss, in particular, your **V**ocational **S**ubject **G**roupings.
★ Analyse your individual contribution and personal performance.
★ Evaluation involves looking at and judging the quality of an activity and asking yourself if you achieved your goals. Consider the following:
  - How and why do we evaluate?
  - Evaluate an activity.
  - Evaluate group performance/teamwork.

SAMPLE EXAM QUESTIONS

These questions are mostly based on this unit only. In the written paper there may be questions which assess a few units together.

Q.1 Voluntary organisations play an increasingly significant role in society.
(a) Name three voluntary organisations in your local area.
(b) Outline the work of one of the organisations you mentioned, stating who benefits from the organisation.
(c) Draft a letter, requesting a speaker from one of the organisations to visit your LCVP class. Explain in your letter why you want the speaker to visit.
(d) Outline methods to evaluate this visit, stating why you chose each method.

Q.2 Evaluation is important for voluntary organisations.
(a) Describe a voluntary organisation indicating, in particular, how it is run, how it is financed and who benefits from it.
(b) Explain the differences between voluntary organisations and business enterprises.
(c) Indicate the importance of evaluation for voluntary organisations and write a brief evaluation of the voluntary organisation you described above. Include five distinct headings.
(d) Outline the benefits of a voluntary organisation to the local community.

Q.3 As an LCVP student, you need to be aware of a range of voluntary organisations.
(a) State the challenges facing voluntary organisations and suggest how they can overcome them.
(b) List the benefits of planning for a voluntary organisation.
(c) Suggest LCVP activities that could help voluntary organisations.
(d) Describe two Leaving Certificate subjects and explain how they were useful for this activity.

Q.4 Enterprising people can also be found in voluntary organisations.
(a) Name a person who holds a senior position in a voluntary organisation and identify the enterprising qualities this person has.
(b) Describe the disadvantages of voluntary organisations.
(c) Draft a short report on a voluntary organisation you investigated as part of the LCVP. In the main body of the report ensure that you include three suitable headings.

Q.5 The people in your locality have joined together to form a community organisation.
(a) List the benefits of having a community association in your area and explain how you can become involved in a community association.
(b) Why would local business offer support to this association?
(c) Discuss the benefits of planning to this association.
(d) Write a brief note on how to evaluate such an organisation and explain why evaluation is important.

LINK MODULE 2 – ENTERPRISE EDUCATION

UNIT 4 – AN ENTERPRISE ACTIVITY

This unit provides you with the opportunity to put the skills you have gained in the previous units of the Link Modules into practice. You will be asked to plan, set up and run your own enterprise activities. You could conduct a community survey, hold a charity fund-raiser, publish a newsletter or local tourist guide, organise a school event or set up a mini-company to sell a product or provide a service. The form of enterprise project selected will depend on your aptitudes and interests, as well as the resources available to you in school and in the locality.

SPECIFIC LEARNING OUTCOMES – SLOs

(as listed in the syllabus)

When you have finished working through this unit, you should be able to:

4.1	work co-operatively with others to generate a range of ideas
4.2	prepare a plan for the selected enterprise activity
4.3	identify available resources to support an enterprise activity
4.4	integrate information from a variety of sources including relevant Leaving Certificate subjects
4.5	assess personal and group skills and identify possible training needs
4.6	identify and recruit consultants willing to advise on a selected enterprise activity
4.7	understand the practical importance of market research and marketing mix
4.8	be aware of the concepts of publicity and promotion
4.9	actively participate in group work in a variety of roles – owner, worker, team leader
4.10	take responsibility to ensure that targets are reached
4.11	participate in a review of group performance
4.12	review personal performance in an enterprise activity
4.13	prepare and present a written or verbal report on an enterprise activity
4.14	link the activities in this unit to learning in relevant Leaving Certificate subjects
4.15	evaluate the successes achieved and problems encountered in this unit.

SETTING UP AN ENTERPRISE

As part of this module you are encouraged to set up your own enterprise projects as vehicles of learning. You must **plan**, **set up** and **run** your enterprise activities. Examples of possible enterprise activities include organising a fund-raiser, publishing a newsletter, organising a school event, (e.g. a careers night), producing a local directory, setting up a school credit union or perhaps setting up a mini-company to sell a product or provide a service.

Running an enterprise helps you get used to making decisions and taking responsibility to ensure targets are reached. Planning will also help you to ensure that goals are achieved. You may have to spend extra time on this activity to ensure that it is successful. Continue to use control procedures throughout the project to compare your actual results with planned results to check that you're on target.

Idea Generation

Firstly you must generate an **idea** for your enterprise. You have already studied idea generation – see Unit 1 of Link Module 2. Brainstorming is an excellent way to come up with ideas. It's important to generate as many ideas as possible, concentrating on **quantity** rather than **quality**. During the LCVP try to absorb as many new enterprise ideas as you can. You could keep an 'Ideas Page' in your LCVP folder and use it to record ideas as you encounter them.

Deciding on a Product/Service

- ✿ Develop a new idea.
- ✿ Copy an existing idea.
- ✿ Change an existing idea – develop it or add something to it.
- ✿ Identify a gap in the market: find a need or desire that no other company is addressing.
- ✿ Enter a niche market, i.e. a specialised area.
- ✿ Do some research and development.

Then, you need to **prioritise** your ideas. Your activity must be achievable within the time constraints of the LCVP. You need to ask yourselves whether the group has got the necessary skills to complete this activity successfully. This is a team activity and it is essential that every member of the group can and does contribute. Is there a **demand** for this product/service? Will it be successful? Remember the most innovative ideas do not necessarily guarantee success. Sometimes simple ideas can be the most effective.

Planning Your Enterprise Activity

The enterprise activity provides you with an ideal opportunity to use an **Enterprise/Action Plan** template (see p. 7). Not only is it an excellent way to plan your enterprise activity, but it also provides you with a portfolio entry. Remember, you can submit a plan of your enterprise as well as an Enterprise Report, provided you don't submit the information documented in the plan as part of your Enterprise Report.

Planning and preparing plans is also an excellent life skill because all businesses must

use an Enterprise/ Action Plan template.

prepare a business plan, which is similar to an Enterprise/Action Plan. In your Enterprise Action/Plan you must identify the following:

- **Objectives/Aims**: Include with these a personal objective and remember to relate these objectives to the Enterprise Education Module.

- **Research methods**: Decide on research methods. Research should be an integral part of every activity. Keep the research methods simple and realistic, e.g. it would not be sensible to consider a class trip to France as a method of research because it would waste time and money. The Internet is a cheap and fast option. Remember, you're going to have to get permission from your principal for such research methods as distributing questionnaires. Use at least three different types of research. Once you have done the research, you must **analyse the outcom**e. This will also help you to decide if you should continue with the activity as planned.

- **Action**: You must then decide on what **actions you must take** to achieve the planned enterprise activity.

- **Schedule of time**: At this stage you will decide on your schedule of time. Keep the time frame short and the enterprise activity simple.

- **Resources**: Make a note of the resources you have. Don't forget that people are a valuable resource and you should make sure that every member of the team is actively involved in the activity. Identify any adults who can help you. They don't have to be teachers: consider a visitor to the classroom, an enterprising local person, parents, relations or maybe a contact from your local Enterprise Board.

- **Finance**: Remember you will need some finance to run this activity. You could look for sponsorship or you could recruit investors by selling shares to the team or you could look for external investors. Identify what assets you will require – you may need equipment, raw materials etc. Are school facilities available and at what cost?

- **Evaluation methods**: Finally, to complete your plan you need to document your evaluation methods, which must relate back to your aims. You may include feedback as an evaluation method. Reflection and evaluation are important because they help you to make better decisions.

Once you have planned your activity, you and your team must be careful not to stray from your plan. All members of the team should be encouraged to get actively involved. Make sure that everybody has a turn at playing each role. It's especially important that each member of the team experiences the role of leader. Make sure that everybody participates in every task, if possible. You may decide to prepare a **SWOT** analysis of your enterprise; this will identify challenges/weaknesses and will help you to decide whether or not you require training or advice. Carrying out an individual and/or team **skills audit** will help to identify any training that is required. Avail of all the help you can get and seek advice from adults and agencies that you encountered during the LCVP.

Revise SWOT analysis.

Revise skills audit.

MARKETING

Marketing is the term used to describe **all aspects** of selling goods and services: from market research to purchasing raw materials, to producing the product, to selling and distributing the product or service, to after-sales service. Marketing identifies, anticipates and satisfies consumers' needs, whilst still making a profit. Your own experience of setting up and running your own enterprise will provide you with an ideal opportunity to put marketing ideas into practice.

Market Research

Market research is an important element of marketing. Market research is the gathering and analysing of information related to your product/service. It is used to discover the needs and wants of customers as well as other important information. Running an enterprise activity provides you with an ideal opportunity to understand the importance of market research and to apply the marketing mix concept. You will need to conduct your own market research before you embark on your enterprise activity by, for example, designing and distributing questionnaires. Then, you will need to consider the practical importance of the marketing mix by using it to sell your product/service.

Reasons for Market Research

- Market research is used to **identify** the types of people interested in a particular product/service.
- Market research is used to find out what **potential customers** need and want.
- It is used to test whether **advertising** is effective.
- It can help the producers to find a suitable **selling price**.
- It is used to investigate **competitors**, i.e. to find out about their strengths, weaknesses and prices.
- Market research can help determine what standard of **quality** the producer should try to achieve.
- It **reduces** the **risks** associated with business and helps to ensure that the business is successful.

Market research reduces the risks associated with introducing and developing products/services.

Types of Market Research

DESK RESEARCH (Secondary)	FIELD RESEARCH (Primary)

This type of research involves finding information that has already been **published**. Sources include:
- Newspapers
- Central Statistics Office
- Internet
- Magazines, trade journals
- Golden Pages
- Reports from
  - Government Departments
  - Chambers of Commerce
  - City and County Enterprise Boards
	This type of research involves going out into the marketplace and **interviewing** customers and potential customers. It involves:
	- Collecting information
	- Questionnaires
	- Observation
	- Personal interviews
	- Telephone interviews
	- Consumer panels
	- Retail audits

QUESTIONNAIRE

A questionnaire must be carefully designed so that it is easy to understand. It also needs to go into enough detail to get the required information. Before you design a questionnaire, brainstorm what information you need to get from the people who'll be filling it out.

Guidelines for Designing a Questionnaire

Tip: What information is required? Draft suitable questions to obtain this information.

- Use clear headings and instructions, e.g. *tick (✓) the appropriate box.*
- Leave a clearly marked space for answers.
- Number questions.
- Each question must be clear and easy to understand.
- Keep the questionnaire short and simple.
- Test out the questionnaire on a small number of people.
- You would usually include a question on personal details and price.
- Avoid leading questions (questions that already suggest the answer) and limit open questions (questions that do not clearly direct the respondent). Multiple choice questions are effective.
- The **sample** is the group of people who complete the questionnaire. A sample should be representative of the total population, so you need to question people of different ages, from different backgrounds etc. The bigger the sample the more accurate the results, but the greater the costs.
- Information needs to be collected quickly and correctly.
- Once you have got the information, it's important that it is analysed properly.

Types of Questions

1. **Dichotomous Questions/Closed Questions/Direct Response Questions**
   The respondent (the person filling out the questionnaire) is asked for a simple response, e.g. Yes/No. The answers are easy to count and categorise.
   Please tick (✓) the appropriate box
   Question: Do you like music? Yes ☐   No ☐

2. **Multiple Choice Questions**
   The respondent is asked to answer a, b, c, d or e. Again, the answers are easy to count and categorise.
   Please tick (✓) the appropriate box
   Question: How often are you paid?
   (a)Weekly ☐   (b)Fortnightly ☐   (c)Monthly ☐   (d)Contract ☐   (e)Other ☐

3. **Open-ended Questions**
   In the case of an open-ended question, the respondent has an opportunity to give his/her own opinion. These answers are difficult to count and categorise because they may contain many different ideas and bring up lots of issues, but they are extremely informative. Ideally you should have one open-ended question in your questionnaire.

   What do you think about our product?

   _____

Remember one very important aspect of conducting a survey is designing the **right questions.**

ACTIVITY

DESIGN A QUESTIONNAIRE

Design a questionnaire for **Gorgeous Gardens**. Consider the following:

★ What **information** do you need to get?
★ Think of **suitable questions** to ask to get this information from the people filling out the questionnaire.
★ Select the most **relevant questions**.

CASE STUDY – GORGEOUS GARDENS LTD

Gorgeous Gardens Ltd, located in Navan, wishes to beautify gardens with their chunky garden furniture. These products are of excellent quality with outstanding workmanship. Ensuring customer satisfaction is the primary goal of Gorgeous Gardens Ltd. Their products consist mostly of garden swings, picnic tables and garden benches with a variety of finishes. Products range in price from €200 to €1,000.

1. List information required.	2. Draft appropriate questions.

ACTIVITY

EVALUATE THE ACTIVITY

1. Did the LCVP class work well as a **team**?
2. Was the **brief** given carried out properly?
3. How well was the **questionnaire** drawn up?
4. How **well-organised** was the administration of the questionnaire, i.e. distribution, collection, publicity, response rate.
5. **Time management** – how long did it take? Did we meet our deadlines?
6. How were the results **counted** and **categorised**?
7. Did it cause **disruptions** in the school?
8. Were there any other **problems?** How did we overcome them?

Gorgeous Gardens Ltd
Athlumny Road, Navan

Garden Furniture

Please tick (✓) the appropriate box.

1. What is your gender?
    Male ☐

    Female ☐

2. Which age group are you in?
    (a) 20–35 ☐   (b) 35–55 ☐   (c) 55 + ☐   (d) Other ☐

3. Would you buy garden furniture?
    Yes ☐   No ☐

4. Which type of garden furniture would you be interested in purchasing?
    Garden ☐   Swing ☐   Picnic Table ☐   Garden Bench ☐   Other ☐
    Please specify_____

5. Which finish would you prefer on your garden furniture?
    Dark ☐   Mahogany ☐   Medium Dark ☐   Chestnut Brown ☐
    Light Green ☐   Other ☐
    Please specify_____

6. How much would you be willing to spend on garden furniture?
    €200–€300 ☐   €301–€400 ☐   €401–€500 ☐   Other ☐

7. Any other comments _____

    _____

Thank you for taking the time to complete our questionnaire.

Identify the **types of questions** in the above questionnaire. Once you have designed your questionnaire, you must then decide how you will distribute the questionnaire, e.g. by post, telephone, e-mail or by interviewing. You must also decide on the number of people you wish to survey.

THE MARKETING MIX

The marketing mix is about getting the 4 P's, i.e. product, price, place and promotion, correct, in order to successfully sell the product/service.

MARKETING MIX 4 P's	
Product	✪ Produce the right product/service. ✪ Design the product/service to suit consumer needs and wants. ✪ Ensure excellent quality. ✪ Develop an ideal brand, promoting an outstanding image, e.g. Levi's. ✪ Ensure the packaging enhances the product and is appropriate. ✪ Having a USP – Unique Selling Point – ensures your product/service has a competitive advantage.
Price	✪ Choose the most suitable price for the product. ✪ You must cover all costs, whilst yielding a sufficient profit. ✪ The price may be determined by demand for the product/service. ✪ You must take competitors' prices into account. ✪ Prices may change from time to time, e.g. during sales.
Place	✪ Identify your market and choose the most appropriate way to distribute your product/service to it. There are different ways of getting the product/service from you to the consumer: – Manufacturer > wholesaler > retailer > customer – Manufacturer > wholesaler > customer – Manufacturer > customer
Promotion	✪ Choose the most appropriate promotion techniques to increase or encourage sales. ✪ Use sales promotions – these are gimmicks used to encourage customers to buy products/services, e.g. 10% extra free, special offers, loyalty cards and points. ✪ Advertise in newspapers, on the radio, or on TV, making sure that you reach your target market. ✪ Personal selling, e.g. sales people, can be effective. ✪ Public relations (PR) promotes awareness of the product to the general public.

Note: Package and personnel may also be identified as additional 'P's' in the marketing mix.

Marketing Mix Case Study

Case Study – Myona Music

Myona Music is a successful enterprise, which was established by two highly motivated and enterprising students from Presentation De La Salle College, Bagenalstown, Co. Carlow. Amy Ryan and Rhona McGarvey are the two people who set up Myona Music.

Their innovative idea was to produce a music booklet with an accompanying tape or CD. All of the songs on the tape or CD can be played at a slow or normal speed, enabling people to learn to read, listen and play the tin whistle. The idea was based on both the Suzuki method (listening and playing by ear) and the classical method (reading musical notes) for the tin whistle.

Myona Music's success was due to their excellent marketing. They did extensive market research and identified a gap in the market. They devised a marketing strategy to create a product and service to win over their customers, both teachers and students.

They carefully put the right marketing mix of product, price, place, promotion and personnel together.

The product was a music booklet with an accompanying tape/CD while the service consisted of workshops that could be arranged to enhance the learning of music. The price was decided on after extensive market research. The price was determined by the unit cost, the level of demand, the competition and the target market. The price varied from €20 to €15 with bulk discounts.

Due to the nature of the product/service, they sold in the following places: craft fairs, primary schools, newsletters, and through their websites. They used every opportunity to promote their product/service, e.g. launches, leaflets and window displays. They came up with a brand name, Myona Music, and then developed a brand image using their local GAA colours, yellow and black, in their promotional activities. The personnel was made up of two students who were enthusiastic about music and who combined their hobby (music) with an enterprise activity. They also created the 'Myona Music Top Ten Tips' for learning the whistle, reminding people that practice makes perfect! They opted for clear packaging so that potential customers could see their booklet and tape/CD.

Their success was due to their extensive and ongoing market research.

Using the above Case Study, document the marketing mix for Myona Music.

Myona Music – Marketing Mix

Product:

Price:

Place:

Promotion:

PROMOTION

Promotion encourages customers to buy goods/services. There are basically four methods of promotion: personal selling, advertising, sales promotion and public relations. The combination of these methods is called the promotional mix.

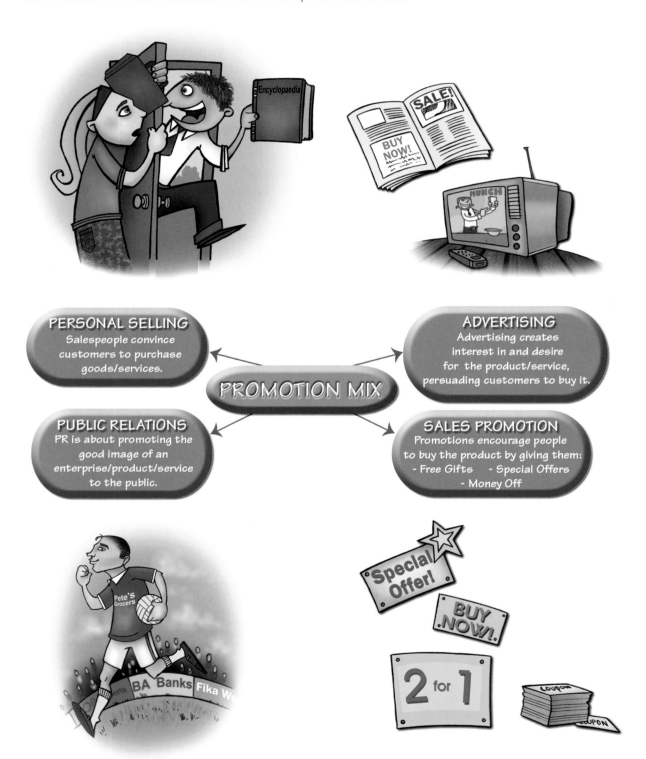

PERSONAL SELLING
Salespeople convince customers to purchase goods/services.

ADVERTISING
Advertising creates interest in and desire for the product/service, persuading customers to buy it.

PROMOTION MIX

PUBLIC RELATIONS
PR is about promoting the good image of an enterprise/product/service to the public.

SALES PROMOTION
Promotions encourage people to buy the product by giving them:
- Free Gifts   - Special Offers
- Money Off

Advertising

Advertising communicates information about a product/service with a view to persuading customers and potential customers to buy the business's product/service.

Reasons for Advertising

- Advertising attracts **attention**.
- It inspires **interest**.
- It develops a **desire**.
- It achieves **action**, i.e. it persuades the customer to purchase the product/service.

Forms of Advertising

- Television   - Radio   - Magazines   - Newspapers   - Cinema   - Billboards
- The Internet   - Shopping bags   - Sponsorship   - Competitions

Planning an Advertising Campaign

When **planning an advertising campaign**, it is important to:
- Have clear **objectives**.
- Decide on a **budget**.
- Choose an **appropriate form** of advertising.
- Decide on an **advertising agency** or appoint an **advertising manager**.
- Decide on a **target market**.

Remember, advertising will only be successful if your campaign is carefully planned.

After the campaign, **evaluate** to see:
- What worked well?
- What aspects were cost effective?
- What would we do differently?

How can you **evaluate**?
- Identify the costs involved and see if the campaign was effective.
- Survey the public.
- Check if sales have shown a significant increase.
- Ask employees for their opinions.

ACTIVITY

Plan an advertising campaign for an organisation of your choice. Use an Enterprise/Action Plan template.

PORTFOLIO ITEM: ENTERPRISE REPORT

The **Enterprise Report** is an optional item in the portfolio. It is a report on an **enterprise activity** in which you have participated during the course of the LCVP. As part of Link Module 2, Enterprise Education, you must **plan, set up** and **run** your own **enterprise projects as vehicles of learning.**

There are many possibilities for this enterprise activity. Take into consideration the **time constraints** (the limited amount of time available to do the project). Examples may include:

* ★ Organising a fund-raiser for a local charity.
* ★ Organising a careers evening.
* ★ Organising a sports activity for juniors.
* ★ Organising sponsorship for sports gear in your school.
* ★ Producing and selling a product or service.

> Tip:
> **Brainstorm** ideas for an enterprise activity.

Things to keep in mind

* ★ Optional: As part of your portfolio you must present a total of six items. The Enterprise Report is part of the **optional** items, unless you decide to submit your Enterprise Report as a Summary Report (core item).
* ★ Your report must be presented as a word-processed document (1,000–1,500 words long).
* ★ The report **must be** the result of a **group activity**, but it must also be your own unique record of that activity.
* ★ Use simple language, short sentences and short paragraphs.
* ★ Arrange information under clear headings and sub-headings.
* ★ Number pages.
* ★ Use a regular font, such as Times New Roman, size 12pt.
* ★ Keep to a small number of font sizes, e.g. two for different headings.

> **Core**
> Submit all 4
> **Optional**
> Submit 2 out of 4
> A total of **6 portfolio items** must be submitted.

Assessment Criteria - Syllabus

The Enterprise Report will be a report on an enterprise activity in which you have participated. The report will assess your ability to:

* ★ Generate a word-processed document with a clear and consistent layout.
* ★ State the terms of reference of the report or the aims of the activity.
* ★ Summarise the main contents.
* ★ Describe key events.
* ★ Communicate relevant information in appropriate depth and detail.
* ★ Use charts, tables, diagrams and pictures, as appropriate, to support and illustrate main findings.
* ★ Organise points into related groups.
* ★ Arrange main sections in a logical sequence.
* ★ Describe and evaluate personal contribution to the activity.
* ★ Draw conclusions and make recommendations appropriate to the body of the report.

Enterprise Report: Guidelines for Report Structure

1. **Title Page**
   - A clear **title**, e.g. 'An Enterprise Report on a fund-raising event for Trócaire' must be included.
   - A **subtitle** may be included, e.g. 'Organised by 5th year LCVP students'.
   - **Author's name**, i.e your name should be included.
   - **For the Attention of**, i.e. mark it for the attention of your teacher.
   - **Date**: date of completion, e.g. 20 January 2006 should be noted.

2. **Table of Contents**
   - List of main sections
   - Page numbers; these must be accurate

3. **Summary**: This should give you a synopsis of the report. Include the following:
   - Subject/main items
   - Main conclusions/recommendations

4. (a) **Terms of Reference**: These explain why the report was written.
   Or

   (b) **Aims of Activity**: Explain what you/your class hoped to learn from the activity. Include three aims and at least one personal aim.

5. **Body of the Report**
   - Key details about your enterprise activity should be described here.
   - Remember the **PEP** approach – **P**re-experience, **E**xperience, **P**ost-experience.
   - Arrange information in a logical sequence under clear headings and subheadings.
   - Small tables may be included in the body of text.
   - Personal contribution: You need to talk about your personal contribution to the enterprise activity. You can do this in one of three ways:
     - You can include a paragraph called 'My Personal Contribution' in the body of the report.
       Or
     - You can highlight your personal contribution in *italics* right through.
       Or
     - You can include an overview of your contribution in your evaluation at the end.

6. **Conclusions**: Your conclusions must relate to the body of the report.

7. **Recommendations**: These are suggestions for future action based on conclusions. Present these as a numbered or bulleted list.

8. **Evaluation**
   - Activity: To what extent were the **aims** achieved?
   - Group evaluation: Evaluate the performance of the group.
   - If not dealt with separately, evaluate your personal contribution.

9. **Appendices (Maximum of two items)**
   There should be at least **one** chart, table, diagram or picture to support the main findings of the report.

Enterprise Report: Possible Template for Rough Work

Title:

Subtitle:

Author's name:

For the Attention of:

Date:

Table of Contents

Summary

Aims

Body of Report

Enterprise Report:
Possible Template for Rough Work

(Body of Report Continued)

Conclusions

Recommendations

Evaluation

    (a) Activity:

    (b) Group Performance:

Appendices (Maximum 2 items)

    1.   2.

An Outline of an Enterprise Report Mind Map

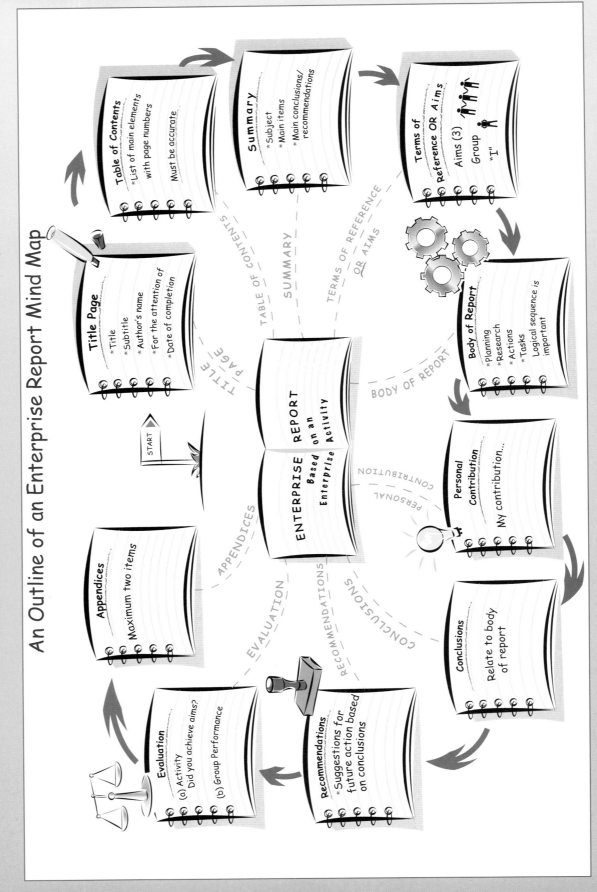

START

Title Page
* Title
* Subtitle
* Author's name
* For the attention of
* Date of completion

Table of Contents
* List of main elements with page numbers

Must be accurate

Summary
* Subject
* Main items
* Main conclusions/ recommendations

Terms of Reference OR Aims

Aims (3)
Group
"I"

Body of Report
* Planning
* Research
* Actions
* Tasks
Logical sequence is important

ENTERPRISE REPORT
Based on an Enterprise Activity

Personal Contribution
My contribution...

Conclusions
Relate to body of report

Recommendations
* Suggestions for future action based on conclusions

Evaluation
(a) Activity
Did you achieve aims?
(b) Group Performance

Appendices
Maximum two items

TITLE PAGE
TABLE OF CONTENTS
SUMMARY
TERMS OF REFERENCE OR AIMS
BODY OF REPORT
PERSONAL CONTRIBUTION
CONCLUSIONS
RECOMMENDATIONS
EVALUATION
APPENDICES

SAMPLE PORTFOLIO ITEM

ENTERPRISE REPORT

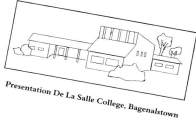

An LCVP enterprise activity by LCVP students in order to raise money to subsidise the cost of school sports gear.

Author:

Marisa Hutchinson Doyle

For the Attention of:

Mr Liam McLaughlin, LCVP teacher

Date:

12 January 2005

Presentation De La Salle College, Bagenalstown

ENTERPRISE REPORT

SAMPLE PORTFOLIO ITEM

Summary

The following is a report on a fund-raiser organised by LCVP students. The report outlines the aims and objectives, planning, preparation, and organisation of this enterprise activity. After extensive research we decided to organise a fund-raising activity to subsidise the cost of sports gear for our school. We decided to sell All Star nominees for €2, for an All Star hurling and an All Star football team. We achieved our aims and evaluated the activity, which was definitely a success as we raised more money than we could have hoped for.

Our excellent teamwork, amazing research, careful planning and immense organisation were all contributing factors. We would also recommend this as an excellent enterprise activity achievable within the time constraints.

Terms of reference

This report was written to ensure that we fulfil the requirements of the LCVP portfolio of an enterprise activity.

Aims and Objectives

The aim was to work together as a team to plan and run an enterprise activity. We hoped to achieve the following:

- To run a successful enterprise activity that's achievable within the time constraints of th
- We hoped to raise €6,000, in order to subsidise the cost of sports gear.
- I hoped to develop both my interpersonal and intrapersonal skills during this activity, improve these skills by working as part of a team and also by working by myself.

Planning

As a class we brainstormed for enterprising ideas to run a fund-raiser. After an idea generation session, we decided to split up into groups to take our ideas further. There were many ideas such as quizzes or raffles but we wanted something different! We knew that people would be attracted if they were getting something from it themselves. We decided to run an activity in order to subsidise the cost of school sports gear for the students.

Teamwork

As a team we brainstormed for ideas on what fund-raising activity to run. As our school is very involved in sports, we decided that the activity should be related to sports, as it would generate interest among the students. We went to the GAA website, www.gaa.ie, and decided that an idea based on the All Star nominees was our best option. We would give students the option of selling All Star nominees in order to subsidise the cost of their own sports gear. We thought this idea was very enticing to students as the more they put into it, the more they got out of it. We quickly began putting this idea into action.

Research

There was a lot of research that had to be carried out before we began implementing our idea.

- **Permission from the Principal**
  First of all, we had to seek the permission of our school principal. We explained our idea to her and she agreed that this activity was worthwhile. She requested that we would work in conjunction with the school sports facilitator.
- **Support of our LCVP co-ordinator and school sports facilitator**
  We organised a meeting with our school sports facilitator and LCVP co-ordinator. We explained our idea and asked them for their support and guidance throughout the activity.
- **Market Research**
  We decided to engage in research to ensure that there was sufficient interest amongst the students who would partake in the activity. I undertook the challenge of market research. I drew up a questionnaire. I distributed it to a sample group of students. I then gathered, recorded and analysed all the information that I had received. This information showed us that there was a phenomenal amount of interest among the students.

Preparation

- **Preparing Nominee Cards**
  We downloaded the sports All Star nominee cards from the Internet. We decided to print the football on the back of the hurling, to reduce the cost of paper. We numbered each card and organised them into bundles of 20 for easier distribution.
- **Contacting Sports Gear Retailers**
  We wrote letters to various sports gear retailers requesting brochures. We received brochures from five companies and also an offer to send a representative from one of the companies. We graciously accepted this offer and arranged for both our team and our school sports facilitator to meet with the representative.
- **Advertising**
  We decided firstly to let the students know what was happening. We wrote a short piece containing all the necessary information and had it announced over the intercom. We posted fliers on notice boards around the school.

Organisation

We held a meeting between our team and the teachers involved, to make sure everything was going according to plan. We decided on the following issues.

- **How to record information on money raised**
  We decided that a chart would be drawn up for each year. On these charts we would record information such as the students' names, the amount of tickets they had got and the amount of money they had raised.
- **Prizes**
  We decided that the winner of each category, hurling and football, would receive €100 each and that the best seller would receive a sports voucher.
- **Time allowed for the selling of nominee cards**
  We decided that the students would have two weeks to sell the nominee cards.
- **Prices of the gear**
  After receiving quotes for the gear from the sports retailer, we decided to offer the students three options when purchasing the gear.

• Buy just a jacket for €50 – sell 25 cards @ €2 each
• Buy shorts and socks for €30 – sell 15 cards @ €2 each
• Buy both the jacket, shorts and socks for €70 – sell 35 cards @ €2 each

It was important to charge €70 for all three items, instead of €80, as this would act as an incentive to buy.

Students would normally have to bring in €30 for shorts and socks and if they could not sell the nominees they made up the difference themselves. The jackets have also been a success and are more a fashion item worn by a majority of students.

SAMPLE PORTFOLIO ITEM

Ordering the Sports Gear
We requested copies of similar gear from the retailer so that the students could decide what sizes they wanted. We allocated certain times for them to try on the gear and place their orders.

Calculating the winners
When the nominees were returned to us we worked hard as a team to calculate the winners. We calculated the scores, the winners were announced and the prizes were presented.

My Personal Contribution
My personal contribution was carrying out the market research, as we needed information directly from the potential consumers. I did this by producing a questionnaire, which I then distributed to a sample group of students. I then gathered, recorded and analysed the information.

Conclusions
- This enterprise was definitely a success. The planning, market research, organisation and teamwork, all contributed to the success.
- We definitely raised more money than we could ever have hoped for. We raised enough money to comfortably subsidise the cost of sports gear for the students in our school.
- We definitely worked well as a team during this activity.

Recommendations
- I would recommend to anyone undertaking a similar activity, to make a chart of the duties of each team member.
- If I did this activity again, I would look for more sponsorship, so that I would be able to offer better prizes and thereby entice more customers to purchase nominees.
- I feel that if I were to do this enterprise again, I would organise more for the presentation of prizes. I would organise a presentation night with a guest speaker presenting the prizes. I also use this event to display the sports gear and publicise the activity, as it was such a suc

Evaluation
- **Activity**

  This activity (fund-raising to subsidise the cost of sports gear for our school) was definitely a success as we raised more money than we could ever have hoped for and were able to comfortably subsidise the cost of the gear.
- **Teamwork**

  The teamwork was definitely a major contributing factor to the success of this activity. We worked well as a team by using our interpersonal and intrapersonal skills together; we ensured that we made our own personal contribution, whilst also working as a team during the activity. There were some disagreements along the way but we got over these. I feel that these were important because, by resolving them, it allowed us to mix the ideas and opinions of different people to attain the best results possible. Resolving these disagreements also brought our team closer together. We worked together to see each other's points of view and to come to a compromise.

(5)

Appendices

(6)

(209)

LEARNING BOARD

Briefly summarise the main points using key words from the unit.	Something I **learned**…
_____	_____
_____	_____
_____	_____
_____	**Something I found difficult…**
_____	_____
_____	_____
_____	_____
_____	Write a short **Case Study** relating to an LCVP Enterprise Activity.
_____	_____
_____	_____
_____	_____
_____	_____

DEVISE AN EXAM QUESTION

Start with a quotation, perhaps a **S**pecific **L**earning **O**utcome or a sentence from this unit.

_____

(a)

(b)

(c)

Write a **6-sentence presentation** on the marketing mix.

_____
_____
_____
_____
_____
_____
_____

LEARNING BOARD

Can I use this for my **portfolio**? **The portfolio is worth 60%.**	Yes ☐	No ☐

If yes, tick the appropriate box below.

CORE – submit all 4
* ★ Curriculum Vitae ☐
* ★ Career Investigation ☐
* ★ Summary Report ☐
* ★ Enterprise/Action Plan ☐

OPTIONAL – submit 2 out of 4
* ★ Diary of Work Experience ☐
* ★ Enterprise Report ☐
* ★ Recorded Interview/Presentation ☐
* ★ Report on 'My Own Place' ☐

A total of 6 portfolio items must be submitted.

Now that you've worked through this unit, what are the next steps?

_____

What new **skills** have I acquired?	Did I participate in any **teamwork** activities? If yes, specify.	Useful **Websites** www.business2000.ie Others…

Tasks
* ★ Explain the term market research.
* ★ Discuss advertising and promotions.
* ★ Describe successes and problems encountered in your enterprise activity.
* ★ List advice and consultants available for your enterprise activity.
* ★ Describe the promotional mix.
* ★ Discuss the marketing mix.
* ★ Discuss the planning you engaged in while participating in your enterprise activity.

CROSS-CURRICULAR

Cross-curricular learning refers to activities or themes which are relevant to many subjects across the curriculum, e.g. health and safety is important in Chemistry, Construction Studies, Engineering, Home Economics and Business.

* ★ What Leaving Certificate subjects were useful? _____

* ★ How were they useful? _____

* ★ Were my **V**ocational **S**ubject **G**roupings useful? _____

211

MAKING IT HAPPEN...
PREPARING FOR ASSESSMENT

Assessment ideas based on Enterprise Education
Unit 8 – An Enterprise Activity

Portfolio of coursework – 60%

Core

★ **Enterprise/Action Plan**
- Plan an enterprise activity.
★ **Summary Report**
- Write a summary report on an enterprise activity, provided you don't submit an Enterprise Report in the options.

Options

★ **Enterprise Report**
★ **Recorded Interview/Presentation**
(a) General interview: 1–2 questions on your enterprise activity.
(b) Presentation on an enterprise activity, provided you don't submit an Enterprise Report in the options.

Written Paper – 40%

*Revise the **layout** and **content of your portfolio items**.*

★ Revise the following topics:
- Idea Generation
- Training Needs
- Recruiting Consultants
- Market Research
- Designing a Questionnaire
- Marketing Mix
- Publicity and Promotion
- Teamwork
- How targets are reached

★ Prepare for questions that demonstrate that you have participated in an activity, e.g. an enterprise activity. Don't forget to use the **PEP** approach to structure your answer: **P**re-experience, **E**xperience and **P**ost-experience. Part of the learning cycle of LCVP is planning, participating and evaluating.

★ Cross-curricular learning – what Leaving Certificate subjects were useful and how? Refer, in particular, to your **V**ocational **S**ubject **G**roupings.

★ Analyse your individual contribution and personal performance.

★ Evaluation involves looking at and judging the quality of an activity and asking yourself if you achieved your goals. Consider the following:
- How and why do we evaluate?
- Evaluate your enterprise activity.
- Evaluate group performance/teamwork.

Tip: Use your portfolio as a revision tool for the written paper.

SAMPLE EXAM QUESTIONS

These questions are mostly based on this unit only. In the written paper there may be questions which assess a few units together.

Q.1 Your LCVP class is planning to run an enterprise activity, selling refill pads, pens, pencils and calculators during the school exams.

(a) Design a questionnaire you could use to carry out some market research to find out if the idea is viable.

(b) Why is research important?

(c) Draft a short Enterprise/Action Plan for this enterprise activity, using key words only.

(d) Describe the benefits to your future employer of your participation in an enterprise activity.

Q.2 Enterprise needs to be understood in the broadest possible context.

(a) Describe enterprise in the LCVP.

(b) Identify an organisation that provides help to an enterprise and state some financial benefits the enterprise may receive.

(c) Explain the term 'marketing mix' and apply the marketing mix to an enterprise of your choice.

(d) Market research is an important element of marketing. Compare desk research with field research.

Q.3 Generating the right ideas and using the right advertising to promote your product is essential to the success of any business.

(a) List five methods of generating ideas and describe one method in detail.

(b) Draw up a questionnaire you could use to carry out research on part-time work in your school.

(c) Identify a product/service you wish to promote. Outline an advertising campaign that you might put in place to promote this product/service.

(d) Why would it be important to evaluate the campaign? Explain how you could carry out an evaluation of the advertising campaign.

Q.4 Starting your own enterprise can be risky, but rewarding.

(a) Explain briefly the advantages of setting up your own business.

(b) Outline important factors that can help to ensure that a business is successful.

(c) Identify personal risks and business risks associated with setting up your own business.

(d) Discuss how you can ensure that the targets of a business are met.

Q.5 Enterprise faces many challenges.

(a) Why would a business engage in training?

(b) Discuss the benefits of teamwork and the skills involved in ensuring that a team works well together.

(c) Outline the challenges facing businesses.

(d) Describe the factors a business would consider prior to employing people and explain why these factors are important.

SECTION 4 - ASSESSMENT

Finally, we must prepare for the assessment. This section offers additional guidelines and practical advice. **Keep a copy of your portfolio and use it as a revision tool for the written paper. Read through your portfolio the night before the written paper and, if you get a chance, read it again on the morning of the exam.** Your portfolio will help you to answer some of the questions, so make sure that you are very familiar with the **content** and the **layout** of each of the portfolio items.

To achieve a distinction can be difficult, so it's extremely important to revise and prepare for the assessment. The general questions will be based on the activities you participated in during the LCVP. The **PEP** (**P**re-experience, **E**xperience and **P**ost-experience) approach demonstrated in this book will help you to structure your experience of LCVP activities and get the most out of them, whilst recording both the knowledge and skills gained. It is important that you take ownership of the activities and take responsibility for your own learning.

Make sure that you are familiar with all the **SLOs** (**S**pecific **L**earning **O**utcomes) and also make sure that you use the knowledge you've gained through your **V**ocational **S**ubject **G**roupings and other Leaving Certificate subjects.

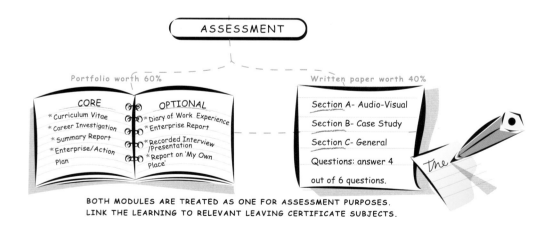

BOTH MODULES ARE TREATED AS ONE FOR ASSESSMENT PURPOSES.
LINK THE LEARNING TO RELEVANT LEAVING CERTIFICATE SUBJECTS.

AN OVERVIEW OF ASSESSMENT

The **two** Link Modules, Preparation for the World of Work and Enterprise Education, are treated as one unit for assessment purposes and the assessment is at a **common level**. On completion of the programme you must present **evidence** to show that you have achieved the SLOs.

Learning will be assessed in the following ways:

1. Terminal Examination Paper - 40% of total marks			
Date	Assessed at the end of the final year of the LCVP		
Duration	2.5 hours		
Content	Section A	Audio-visual presentation	30
	Section B	Case Study (Received in advance.)	30
	Section C	General questions (4 x 25 marks) (Answer four out of six.)	100
TOTAL MARKS			160

2. Portfolio of Coursework - 60% of total marks			
Date	Assessed at the end of the final year of the LCVP		
Duration	Assembled over the two years of the programme		
Content	1. **Core Items** (All 4 items to be presented.)	(a) Curriculum Vitae (b) Career Investigation (c) Summary Report (d) Enterprise/Action Plan	25 40 40 35
	2. **Optional Items** (2 out of 4 items to be presented.)	(a) Diary of Work Experience (b) Enterprise Report (c) Recorded Interview/Presentation (d) Report on 'My Own Place'	50 50 50 50
TOTAL MARKS			240

Total Marks: 400 for both the written exam and the portfolio

Certification

LCVP students receive the same certificate as students of the established Leaving Certificate. An additional statement of the grade received for the Link Modules is applied to the certificate.

Grades for the Link Modules are awarded as follows:

> 1. Distinction: 80–100%
> 2. Merit: 65–79%
> 3. Pass: 50–64%

Points

LCVP students have the same opportunity to proceed to universities and other third level institutions as students of the established Leaving Certificate. The Link Modules are presently recognised in terms of points as follows:

Universities, DIT and Institutes of Technology

> Distinction: 70 points
> Merit: 50 points
> Pass: 30 points

Note: The State Examinations Commission issues guidelines each year that highlight any changes in assessment.

EXAM

The written paper takes place in May of the Leaving Certificate year. It makes up 40 per cent of the total marks. Remember to use the portfolio as a tool for revision. Revise both the layout and the content. Sections A and B are compulsory, which means that you must answer both the Audio-visual and Case Study questions.

Attempt every part of every question you answer and don't leave blank spaces. Use headings and subheadings and define your answer, elaborate on it and, if appropriate, support it with examples. Don't waffle and if for some reason you run out of time, write down key words.

Section A: Audio-Visual Presentation (30 Minutes)

You should be familiar with the format of this section from using past papers with the video tapes. First of all, **read the questions** and decide what information is required. While watching the video, **take notes** on the rough-work page in your exam answer booklet and remember that you may be asked questions about **what you see** as well as about **what you hear**. There are normally **eight questions**. Note the marks attached to each question. Remember to answer the last two questions in detail, as they carry 12 out of 30 marks. Don't forget to elaborate. Give examples, if appropriate, and supply any relevant information you encountered during the programme.

Section B: Case Study (25 Minutes)

Remember, you get this Case Study four weeks before the examination. Use the method for preparing the Case Study explained in this book (see p. 224). Make sure you know your Case Study and have an in-depth understanding of all aspects of it. Read the questions carefully. Stop and think, *What exactly is being asked?* The questions on the written paper may not be the questions you anticipated.

Section C: General Questions (4 x 23 Minutes)

This section contains six questions and you should answer any four. To assist you in choosing and locating questions, the exam paper has a **summary and index of questions**. Skim through all of the questions and then choose which questions you will answer. Read the questions you have chosen carefully and then start by answering the easiest question. Allow 23 minutes approximately per question. Don't spend extra time on your favourite question. Make sure that your answers have sufficient detail and be aware of the marks for each part of the question.

Always define your answer, explain your answer and, if possible, give an example supporting your answer.

Don't leave blank spaces – attempt all parts of the questions. Make sure you are familiar with the layout of the answer booklet in which you write your answers. The answer booklet leaves adequate spaces for answers.

THE PORTFOLIO OF COURSEWORK

A portfolio is a purposeful collection of your work that exhibits your efforts, progress and achievements. The purpose of the LCVP portfolio is to demonstrate the depth and breadth of your skills and capabilities through examples of your work. The portfolio is generated over a two-year period and you're encouraged to re-visit and revise your work. It should represent a collection of your **best work**. It must be prepared in accordance with specific criteria and provide evidence that you have planned, participated in and learned from a variety of activities organised as part of the Link Modules.

The content of the portfolio must relate to the syllabus, in particular to the **S**pecific **L**earning **O**utcomes (**SLOs**) and must be presented in accordance with the assessment criteria and important guidelines.

You must submit **six pieces** of work for the LCVP portfolio. This makes up 60 per cent of your final mark in the Link Modules. There are **four** compulsory core items: a Curriculum Vitae, a Career Investigation, a Summary Report and an Enterprise/Action Plan. You must also submit any **two** of the four optional items: a Diary of Work Experience, an Enterprise Report, a 'My Own Place' Report and a Recorded Interview/Presentation.

The portfolio of coursework is worth 60 per cent.

Compulsory (Core): all four	1. **Curriculum Vitae** 2. **Enterprise/Action Plan** 3. **Career Investigation** 4. **Summary Report**
Options: any two	5. **Diary of Work Experience** 6. **Enterprise Report** 7. **'My Own Place' Report** 8. **Recorded Interview/Presentation**

Submit 6 pieces only.

Your completed portfolio should represent your best work.

It's your responsibility to select which **items** to include in your portfolio. They must be your **own work**.

Your teacher will advise you on any changes in the **guidelines** issued by the examining authority.

Portfolio: NCCA Recommendations

PORTFOLIO PRESENTATION	RESTRICTIONS
- Present on **A4 paper** in a soft covered folder. - Your **examination number** must be included on cover. - It's acceptable to include your name on any/all items. - Should have a **contents page** with a list of items submitted. - If you opt for the audio recording in the Career Investigation and/or the Recorded Interview/Presentation, it must be clearly stated on your contents page. - Each portfolio item should have a clear title, i.e. Curriculum Vitae, Enterprise Action Plan etc. - You should use a regular font size and type, e.g. 12pt Times New Roman for all body text. - Margin of 1 to 1.5 inches should be used.	- You can't have **duplication.** - You may not submit a Summary Report on a Career Investigation. - If you submit an Enterprise Report (options), you may not submit a Summary Report (core) on this activity. - If you submit a 'My Own Place' Report in options, you may not submit a Summary Report on the same activity. - If you submit a Diary of Work Experience in the options, you may not submit a Summary Report on the same activity. - If you submit a Recorded Interview/Presentation, you may not submit a Summary Report on the same activity. - However, you may prepare an Enterprise/Action Plan for any activity already reported on in the portfolio, provided the plan is not reproduced in that report or diary. - The content of the Career Investigation and the Summary Report or any other optional item may not be the principal topic of your Recorded Interview/Presentation. An activity already reported on by you should not account for more than 25 per cent of the Recorded Interview.
PORTFOLIO CONTENT	RESTRICTIONS
- You must only submit material generated as a result of Link Modules activities in which you participated. - 6 items only are to be presented. - Each item must be your original work. - Inclusion of material directly downloaded or copied from other sources is not acceptable. - Portfolio items should relate to a number of separate activities.	Remember the **portfolio is exam material** and the integrity of the examination process must be protected. Produce your own items for the portfolio. Any exemplar material is only a guide to style but not to content. Your results can be withheld if work presented is similar, which can give rise to suspicions of copying.

Portfolio: Comparison of Reports

Summary Report (Core): 300-600 Words	Enterprise Report (Optional): 1,000-1,500 Words	Report On 'My Own Place' (Optional): 1,000-1,500 Words
Title: Author:	Title Page: Title: Author: Intended audience: Date of completion:	Title Page: Title: Author: Intended audience: Date of completion:
	Table of Contents ○ List of main sections ○ Page numbers	Table of Contents ○ List of main sections ○ Page numbers
	Summary: synopsis	Introduction: description, aspect, map
Terms of reference or aims – Group and Personal "I"	Terms of reference or aims – Group and Personal "I"	Terms of reference or aims – Group and Personal "I"
Body Short sentences Short paragraphs Headings, sub-headings Bullet points Chronological order May contain tabulated information	Body Key details of enterprise Headings, sub-headings Bullet points Relevant illustrations – at least 1 Evidence of personal contribution	Body Main findings of investigation Headings, sub-headings Bullet points Relevant illustrations – at least 1 Evidence of personal contribution Out-of-school activity described Research methods Local issue analysed Link learning to at least 2 Leaving Certificate subjects
Conclusions – relate to aims Recommendations – based on conclusions	Conclusions – relate to body Recommendations – based on conclusions	Conclusions – relate to aims Recommendations – based on conclusions
	Evaluation ○ Activity ○ Group Performance	Evaluation ○ Investigation ○ Group Performance
No Appendices	Appendices Maximum 2 items	Appendices Maximum 2 items

Possible Marking Scheme for Core Portfolio Items (All 4 must be submitted)

MAXIMUM 140 MARKS

1 Curriculum Vitae

Word-processing	1–2
Presentation and layout (conventional order)	1–3
Personal details (any 4 items, including signature)	0–4
Skills and qualities	0–2
Educational qualifications	0–3
Work experience	0–3
Achievements/interests/hobbies	0–5
Referees	0–3
Sub-total	**25**

2 Enterprise/Action Plan

Presentation and layout	0–3
Title and purpose	0–2
Objectives (at least 2 needed)	0–4
Research methods	0–2
Analysis of research	0–6
Action steps	0–6
Schedule of time/costs	0–6
Evaluation methods	0–6
Sub-total	**35**

3 Career Investigation

Title, word-processing and use of headings **or** for audio tape: communication in clear and confident manner	0–5
Description of duties involved in the career/area	0–3
Identification of skills and qualities needed	0–5
Identification of qualifications and training needed	0–5
What did you learn about the career and about yourself by doing this research/activity?	0–8
Description of two different pathways to the career	0–4
Evaluation of the career	0–5
Evaluation of undertaking the Career Investigation	0–5
Sub-total	**40**

4 Summary Report

Presentation and layout	1–5
Title and name of activity	0–5
Author's name	0/5
Terms of reference of report/aims of the activity	0/3/5
Body of report – content (short sentences, summaries, appropriate language)	1–10
Body of report – clarity (headings, logical structure, flow, originality of thought)	1–5
Conclusions and recommendations	1–5
Sub-total	**40**

Note: the marking schemes may change.

LCVP Portfolio Marking Scheme reproduced with the permission of the State Examinations Commission.

Possible Marking Scheme for Optional Portfolio Items (2 out of 4 must be submitted)

MAXIMUM 100 MARKS

5 | Record/Log/Diary

Presentation and layout	0-5
Name and description of work experience placement	0-5
Reasons for choosing work experience placement	0-5
Content	
Factual day-to-day account of at least 3 days.	
Insert entries as follows:	
– Detailed personal account	0-10
– Your analysis of your own performance in different situations	0-10
Expression and evaluation	
Evaluation of experience in the light of study and career aspirations	0-5
Evaluation of how the skills acquired can be applied to work in the home, at school and in the local community	0-10
Sub-total	**50**

6 | Report

Presentation and layout	0-4
Title and table of contents	0-2
Author's name or signature	0-2
Terms of reference of report/aims of activity	0-4
Summary of main points	0-4
Body of report (may include personal contribution)	
Account of activity	0-10
Use of appropriate depth, detail with good organisation of information	0-8
Use of charts, tables, diagrams	0-4
Conclusions and recommendations	0-6
Evaluations	0-6
Sub-total	**50**

7 | 'My Own Place'

Presentation and layout	0-4
Title/table of contents	0-2
Description of local area/what is under investigation	0-5
Aim/objectives	0-5
Research methods	0-5
Body of report – description and analysis of key aspects	0-6
Use of logical sequence/headings/illustrations	0-5
Analysis of issue/suggestions for improvements	0-6
Conclusions and recommendations	0-6
Evaluation	0-6
Sub-total	**50**

8 | Recorded Interview/Presentation

Presentation (neat in the context of the interview/presentation)	0-4
Variety of tone, gesture, diction, eye contact	0-4
Ability to communicate message clearly, to engage audience, to elaborate on points/questions, to express a logical sequence of thought	0-36
Pass (18–23) – basis communication skills	
Merit (24–27) – ability to express ideas and opinions clearly with good knowledge of topic	
Distinction (28–36) – good knowledge and ability to communicate ideas and own opinions clearly and in logical sequence.	
Information (content)	0-6
Sub-total	**50**

Note: the marking schemes may change.

Tips for Perfecting your Portfolio Items

You want to achieve full marks and marks will be awarded for presentation. Remember, you are being tested on your word-processing, design and composition skills as well as on the content of your portfolio items.

- Make sure that each portfolio item has a clear **title**.
- The portfolio entries must be word-processed to **perfection** and **error-free**.
- Remember, you have two years to complete your entries. Check carefully for **correct spelling** and **grammar** as there is no excuse for mistakes.
- Check **punctuation** carefully. The rule of thumb is to be **consistent**.
- Use **language** that is simple, accurate and concise.
- Use **short sentences** and **short paragraphs**.
- Use a **regular font** such as Times New Roman, size 12pt.
- Make sure that all headings are exactly the same size and style (e.g. size 14 and bold).
- Keep to a small number of font sizes, e.g. two.
- Use exactly the same **spacing** under each heading. If you leave a space of one line under a heading, make sure you leave a space of one line under all headings.
- **Tabs** are also extremely important and must be consistent.
- Margins of 1–1.5 inches (2.5–3.75cm) should be used.

THE CASE STUDY

The Case Study is a descriptive account of a person, an enterprise (business, community or voluntary), your local area or a socio-economic issue.

The Case Study arrives in your school approximately four weeks before the written exam. When you receive your copy, make good use of the opportunity to understand and analyse it because you will only have approximately 25 minutes to answer questions on it in the exam. Instead of trying to predict what questions will come up in relation to the Case Study, you should use the Case Study as a revision tool for the other questions in the written paper, by applying the **S**pecific **L**earning **O**utcomes. Any **S**pecific **L**earning **O**utcomes relevant to the Case Study could form the basis of a question in the exam, so the only way to cover all of the possibilities is to revise **all** of the **S**pecific **L**earning **O**utcomes while analysing the Case Study. This will help you not just in the Case Study questions but it will also be important revision for the whole written paper. Receiving the Case Study in advance helps to prevent blanks on the day of the exam.

RESOURCES
- ✪ Past exam papers and exam videos
- ✪ Business 2000, www.business2000.ie
- ✪ Newspapers
- ✪ Enterprise Encounter Resource folder (contact Enterprise Boards)
- ✪ Websites
- ✪ Other

Note: You may decide to write your own Case Study based on a Visit In/Visit Out, on voluntary organisations, community enterprises, business enterprises, 'My Own Place', or on enterprise activities, to name a few.

Assessment Criteria – Syllabus

The Audio-visual and Case Study questions on the examination paper will assess your ability to:
- ✪ evaluate essential factual information
- ✪ identify and analyse relevant social and economic factors
- ✪ recognise patterns and link these with knowledge and experiences gained through other LCVP activities
- ✪ propose and/or evaluate solutions to problems
- ✪ express informed opinions on related issues

In the LCVP you are assessed on two Case Studies:
        (a)   Audio-visual Case Study – Section 1 of the written paper
        (b)   Written Case Study – Section 2 of the written paper
Both of these Case Studies are **compulsory** and it's important as part of the LCVP to use Case Studies frequently.

A Method for Preparing for the Case Study

You receive the Case Study in advance of the written exam but you will only receive the questions on the day of the exam. This is an ideal methodology to prepare for the Case Study:

1. **Read** the Case Study.
   (a) Skim read to gain an understanding and a general sense of the Case Study.
   (b) Read a second time and underline the following:
   - (i) **Difficult words**
   - (ii) **Business words**
   - (iii) **LCVP-related words**

   Make sure that you can explain these words with examples, if appropriate. Make sure that you can make three points about the use or significance of these words as there may be a full question on them.

2. Prepare a **SWOT/SCOT** analysis.
   (a) SWOT – Strengths, Weaknesses, Opportunities and Threats
   (b) SCOT– Strengths, Challenges, Opportunities, and Threats

3. **Identify problems** and **make decisions.**
   (a) Use **brainstorming** to list all possible problems.
   (b) What would you do to solve these problems?
   (c) List different courses of action.
   (d) Prioritise problems. Which problems are the most significant and why?

4. Prepare a profile on the following: **people, organisation and place**.
   (a) People: Prepare a profile on qualities, skills and experiences.
   (b) Organisation: Define the type of organisation. Is it a business/community enterprise or a voluntary organisation? Is it a sole trader, partnership or company?
   (c) Place: Does location matter?

5. Prepare a **Summary** and/or **Presentation**. Perhaps you can reduce the first five lines to one line and so on.

To become familiar with Case Studies that have come up in previous years, use exam papers and suggested solutions. You may try and anticipate possible questions, but it's more important to have an **in-depth understanding of the Case Study.**

By using the above methodology and using the Case Study to revise **all** of the **S**pecific **L**earning **O**utcomes, you will have a deeper understanding of it. Then, regardless of what questions come up, you will be able to answer them and suggest appropriate solutions.

How many SLOs can I apply to the Case Study?

Remember that in the assessment you will have to write down the solutions to questions. This is a different skill to oral discussion and it's important to practise it. You should use your LCVP folder throughout the two years to write down what you do, experience and learn. You will then be more used to expressing yourself on paper when it comes to the assessment.

A Method for Preparing for the Case Study

✿ **CASE OVERVIEW**	1. Skim read. 2. Underline words.	Develop a sense of the case. Get a feel for it. – Difficult words – Business words – LCVP-related words
✿ **PREPARE A SWOT ANALYSIS**	1. Strengths 2. Weaknesses 3. Opportunities 4. Threats	
✿ **PROBLEMS**	1. List problems. 2. Prioritise problems.	Solutions *What would 'I' do?* Identify the biggest problem.
✿ **PROFILE**	– People – Place – Organisation	
✿ **SUMMARY** – Reduce the first five sentences to one and so on.		

You may decide to anticipate questions for the written exam but it is more important to have a deep understanding of the Case Study.

Make a note of key words as you analyse the Case Study, and then remember to elaborate on these and give detailed answers in the written exam. **Define your answer, explain your answer and give an example to support it, if appropriate.**

Importance of the Case Study in the LCVP

The Case Study is a valuable learning tool for the following reasons:
- ✿ It makes the LCVP more interesting.
- ✿ It is a useful tool for putting theory into practice.
- ✿ It encourages you to diagnose problems and come up with solutions.
- ✿ It allows you to present your point of view.
- ✿ It can give you a taste of real life.
- ✿ Class discussion of the Case Study will help you to develop listening skills and will help you to understand other people's perspectives.

Teamwork on the Case Study

It is possible to work on the Case Study alone by reading it and using the method for preparing for it highlighted in this section. However, when analysing the Case Study, it's useful to get as many people as possible involved. You won't always have the right answer and other viewpoints can generate interesting ideas. You could **role-play** some aspect of the Case Study and document learning. **Brainstorming** could be used to create lists of strengths, weaknesses etc. Ask other adults for their opinions on the Case Study, e.g. you could ask a business teacher, City and County Enterprise Board etc. The more people involved, the more ideas, opinions and advice you will receive. This should help you develop a greater understanding of the Case Study.

- ✿ **Work in pairs**: Link with a business student if possible.
- ✿ **Work in groups**: Get different groups to concentrate on different aspects, for example:
  - ▬ Group 1 – Strengths
  - ▬ Group 2 – Weaknesses
  - ▬ Group 3 – Opportunities
  - ▬ Group 4 – Threats

Alternatively, different groups could work on profiling people, organisation and place, prioritising problems and applying a number of the **S**pecific **L**earning **O**utcomes.

Case Studies from Past Papers

Section B	Case Study 2005	30 Marks

Community Development

Ballytra is situated 80 kilometres from the nearest city and 20 kilometres from four other large towns. The town has an attractive river running through it with a large oak forest to the west of the town. There is one primary school, a community college and a community training centre located in the town. There is one hotel with sixteen rooms which is in need of refurbishment. A 19th century country house, in need of repair, with a nine hole golf course attached to it is situated 8 kilometres from the town.

Ballytra is home to a company called Choc O'Late Ltd. For the past eight years. This is a confectionery business owned by two brothers. It is situated on an industrial site just outside the town. The company has sixty-five employees. In 2002 the turnover was nine million euro but this has decreased to seven million euro in 2004 due to the lack of demand for confectionery products. Also, increased competition and increases in insurance and wage costs have affected the company. This has led to some employees losing their jobs and the company is now talking of downsizing their business further having conducted an audit of the company's finances.

Due to the job losses in Choc O'Late Ltd. and the lack of continued new employment in the area, local people realised their children would not be in a position to settle down in the town in the future. This jolted them into action and the business community and local people were invited to a public meeting. Here various ideas and proposals were discussed. Several enterprises ideas were put forward which could be developed in the area. The challenges of setting up new business ventures in the town are very significant especially with regard to necessary resources and expertise.

A community development committee was selected to oversee any development initiatives. The intention of the committee is to use a local resource audit to establish the community's resources and strengths and to try to negotiate the establishment of a Business Park with local authorities. Certain members of the committee are highly environmentally conscious and would like to see socially and environmentally responsible businesses set up in their town.

Q.1 What facilities do teenagers require in, or near, their home town? (6 marks)

Q.2 Choc O'Late Ltd is considering downsizing its operations. What alternatives should be considered before this decision is taken? (12 marks)

Q.3 The community development committee decides to draw up a document outlining the attractions of the town for potential enterprises.

(a) Put, in order of priority, your list of advantages of Ballytra and briefly explain each.

(b) What are the disadvantages of a Business Park in the area?

(c) Draw up a list, in order of importance, of the qualities required by the committee in enterprises applying to locate in the proposed Business Park.

(12 marks)

| Section B | Case Study 2004 | 30 Marks |

European Special Games 2004

In conjunction with Ireland's presidency of the E.U. Ireland has been asked to host a special European Games in May 2004. Teams from all existing member states and teams from all the new member states will take part in these games. The games will give an opportunity to those with Special Needs to take part in a variety of sporting events.

The Games will take place during the second week in May. The teams will arrive in the country during the first week of May and they will be staying in towns and cities throughout the country during the first week of their visit. This will allow the teams to settle into Ireland, meet Irish people and prepare to compete. The host towns will be organising events to make the visitors welcome, give them an understanding of our culture and will be providing facilities to help them train and prepare for the games.

The European Special Games will take place in and around Dublin. Ten different venues will be used to facilitate the different sports. The participants, their trainers and helpers will come to Dublin for the week of the games and will stay in hotels and universities across the city. Each day transport will be provided to bring the teams to the events.

The organising committee for the European Special Games have been planning the games for the past 3 years. They began by involving a number of people in different areas such as sponsorship, marketing, accommodation, catering, medical, transport and the competition events themselves. The committees have members who have responsibilities for each area. These members in turn have a team of people to help with the work. As the time of the games draws nearer they will be involving more and more people to ensure that all gets done.

Thousands of volunteers will be needed to help throughout the two weeks that the participants are in Ireland. These helpers will be needed to assist with the teams from when they arrive at the airport to when they leave. Some helpers will be needed in the host towns and cities, others will be needed during the week of the Games themselves to help at the accommodation venues and at the competition venues. Volunteers with a variety of skills, such as language or medical expertise, will be required. Training will be provided for all volunteers in the month before the Games and all volunteers must have obtained Garda clearance before they will be issued with their security passes and uniforms. Volunteers will be assigned to specific duties and can sign up for a number of days depending on their availability.

The event will be covered by national and international media. The formal opening and closing ceremonies will take place in Dublin. All the participants are likely to attend these occasions.

Answer all questions.
Q.1. Outline **three** benefits of hosting the European Special Games for Ireland.
(6 marks)
Q.2. A national advertising campaign invited those interested to help during the two weeks of the games.
(i) Describe in detail **four** reasons why you would consider volunteering
OR
(ii) Describe in detail **four** reasons why you would not consider volunteering.
(12 marks)
Q.3. The organising of these games is a considerable task involving many different people.
(i) Draft an appropriate time plan which the organisers would have used in planning the games.
(ii) Outline **three** important areas which must be included in the **national** plan for the games.
(12 marks)

Section B **Case Study 2003** **30 Marks**

ELECT. Ltd.

Ruth Flynn is 27 years old. She sat her Leaving Certificate nine years ago. She did not know what she wanted to do so she did not apply for college at that time. She began working in a local factory which suited her, as she did not wish to move away from home. At first Ruth worked on an assembly line in MPD Ltd., an electronics factory making car radios and other small electrical goods. Ruth's job was assembling part of the radio as the conveyor belt passed along. She worked in a unit with ten other workers. After three years she was promoted to supervisor of her section. This involved record-keeping on the items produced and planning the week's work for the unit with the production manager. Despite the extra responsibility and extra money that came with her job, Ruth was beginning to get bored and decided to go to college at night. Four years later, she qualified with a degree in Business Administration.

The management in MPD Ltd. recognised that Ruth had talents and abilities and she became assistant manager in charge of purchasing the raw materials. This involved travelling to meet suppliers and planning for what was needed and when it would be needed on a day to day basis. Many of the parts have to be bought from abroad. This has resulted in delays in the delivering of parts for MPD Ltd. and other firms in related industries.

An opportunity arose for an agent in this country to handle the buying of these parts on behalf of several manufacturers. Ruth thought about it and decided that this was the way forward for her. It would suit her personally and business wise. She set up her own company ELECT. Ltd.

There were many decisions to be made and Ruth had to draw up an extensive Business Plan so that she would be able to begin her business. This involved market research in this country to establish who her potential customers might be and also to ascertain what their requirements might be. She also had to carry out research to establish who the suppliers were at present and who could be possible suppliers for new products for customers. She found her local Enterprise Board very helpful.

Because Ruth was setting up an agency she did not need a large manufacturing plant: instead she is the middle person between the supplier and the manufacturer. Much of her work can, and is, done over the phone and internet. ELECT. Ltd. meets with its customers on a regular basis to plan a schedule of what is needed by them and when they require delivery. The customers must have confidence in ELECT. Ltd. that they will supply what is required at the correct time.

Ruth initially employed one person in the office, and later on, a sales person who deals with the customers. Because much of the work is done via internet, Ruth knows that it is important to have an up to date, user friendly web-site. She spent considerable time and money developing the web-site when the company was set up and she updates it regularly. Because the use of the internet in business is expanding, Ruth believes there are many opportunities for her to develop her business.

Answer all questions.
Q.1. State and explain briefly **three** advantages to Ruth of setting up her own business.
(6 marks)
Q.2. Outline **three** major decisions Ruth will have to make to ensure that her business is successful.
(12 marks)
Q.3. Identify **three** personal and **three** business risks associated with business expansion. Explain the implications of each.
(12 marks)

| Section B | Case Study 2002 | 30 Marks |

EntCo

EntCo is a business which operates from a Business Park, located 1 mile from Bailebeg, a town of 5000 inhabitants. Bailebeg is 40 miles from the nearest city and is situated along a motorway. The town had a tradition of textile based industries, but all of these are now closed down. The Business Park has attracted a range of industries, all of which are now successful.

Sister and brother, Maeve and Peter Ryan own and run EntCo. Maeve has a background in Business and Computers. After leaving College, she worked 8 years for firms in Ireland and London. Peter is a qualified chef and, before setting up the business, worked for a large city hotel for 5 years. Peter oversees production and new product development. Maeve has responsibility for the sales and marketing, and administration requirements.

EntCo is involved in the food business. It began as a catering company providing prepared meals for canteens in local businesses. Currently the company uses fresh ingredients in all its products. Ingredients are sourced locally, and, as the fruit and vegetables are readily available, the business does not have a problem obtaining raw materials.

The business has grown over the past two years and now employs 8 full-time and 20 part-time workers. The company aims to be adaptable and will look after customer needs at all times. Maeve is continually looking for new markets and ways to develop the business. As the market for its produce has expanded the company has extended its product range.

Maeve saw an opportunity in the retail sector brought about by the changing lifestyles of customers who demand good quality, convenience food. Maeve and Peter have worked to develop the range of products and to plan how a large number of orders could be met. Now EntCo supplies supermarkets and delicatessens in the area with prepared meals and individual dishes. The company also caters for individual party orders for special functions. This area of the business has expanded rapidly and EntCo now caters for many of the large functions in the area.

Recently, one of the old textile factories has been bought by a food production company which produces a wide range of frozen foods and vegetables. This company has three other large food plants in the country. Maeve and Peter are aware that they must be competitive and offer a unique service. They carry out market research regularly in order to come up with new ideas for products.

EntCo has been approached by a large supermarket chain to supply ready-made, easy cook meals. If Maeve and Peter are to begin supplying this supermarket chain they will have to expand and upgrade their production facility. They have started to draw up a plan so that they can set out the implications of this possible expansion.

Answer all questions.

Q.1. State and explain briefly **three** positive features of EntCo.
      (6 marks)
Q.2. Complete a S.W.O.T. analysis of EntCo.
      (12 marks)
Q.3. (i) Describe how EntCo could overcome possible competition from the large food
          production company which has recently purchased one of the old textile factories.
      (ii) Explain **three** implications for EntCo of proceeding with its expansion plans.
      (12 marks)

| Section B | Case Study 2001 | 30 Marks |

Futura Systems Ltd.

Six years ago Una and Frank set up their own small business, Futura Systems Ltd. Both had worked in the computer industry for 10 years prior to setting up the business. Frank had worked in the Marketing/Public Relations area and Una had worked as a computer programmer. They both had worked for companies that were rapidly expanding. As a result of the expansion of the computer industry, their roles in their respective companies were changing. Both were unhappy with these changes so they decided to set up a business together.

Throughout the 10-year period when they worked for other companies Una and Frank were very aware of the changes taking place in the computer industry. During this time they also built up many contacts in the industry in their own respective specialist areas. They noted the growth in the industry and the changing needs of all those conducting business in the different sectors. In particular, they were aware of the need for Information Technology development by sole traders, businesses of all sizes and other organisations. Una and Frank decided to meet the technology needs of these customers by setting up a business to supply computer systems and customised software packages. These objectives encouraged them to set up Futura Systems Ltd.

Futura Systems Ltd. operates out of a Business Park in the suburbs of a city. The company now employs 25 people and each member of staff is a college graduate. The staff are organised into Project Groups each consisting of five employees. Each group has a technical, software, marketing and financial specialist. Each group totally manages its own orders. Satisfying the customer is seen as being of primary importance.

Over the past few months the business has had problems meeting deadlines for a number of projects. These problems are particularly associated with two of the Project Groups. This has resulted in frustration for some of the employees and the management.

A number of employees have made complaints to the management, as they are frustrated at not being able to do their own work satisfactorily. Frank is particularly worried as he feels that these issues will have an effect on customer service that will have both short-term and long-term implications for the business.

Futura Systems Ltd. operates in an ever-changing environment where it must keep up to date with developments in both the hardware and software areas. At present the top management teams are preparing a long-term plan for the business. Survival in the future is crucial.

Una and Frank are aware that the economy is thriving at present and thus constant research and development must take place if the business is to stay competitive. Una has researched the state agencies that can be of assistance to them in the future and has identified the type of assistance each can offer to the business. Una and Frank as the top management team are reviewing how their business has developed and how it might proceed in the future.

Answer all questions.

Q.1. Describe in detail **three** benefits of organising the workplace into Project Groups?
(6 marks)

Q.2 Identify **three** possible problems which Una and Frank face in the short-term and/or long-term. Suggest a possible way to deal with each problem.
(12 marks)

Q.3. Identify and explain **three** issues which Una and Frank should consider when preparing their long-term plan.
(12 marks)

LCVP ASSESSMENT WORDS

The following terms appear frequently in the general questions in Section C:

Analyse	To study a problem in detail by breaking it down into various parts and examining possible relationships
Apply	To bring knowledge or skills into use for a particular purpose
Comment on	To express an opinion about something
Compare	To examine two or more things in order to discover their similarities
Contrast	To show the difference/s between
Criterion	A standard by which something can be judged or decided
Characteristics	Distinguishing qualities or attributes of an individual or object
Define	To state the precise meaning of
Describe	To give an account of a person, relationship, event, organisation or location
Draft	To draw up a document, letter, report
Evaluate	To find or determine the worth, value or significance of something; to assess or make a judgement
Explain	To make clear in a detailed manner
Identify	To show recognition of something
Illustrate	To make clear by means of examples, charts, diagrams, etc.
Indicate	To point out or state briefly
List	To write down a number of names or objects having something in common
Mention	To refer to briefly
Outline	To give a short summary of the important features of a subject
Qualities	The distinguishing characteristics or attributes of an individual or object
Suggest	To put forward an idea or plan